WASHINGTON COUNTY MURDER & MAYHEM

WASHINGTON COUNTY MURDER & MAYHEM

HISTORIC CRIMES OF SOUTHWESTERN PENNSYLVANIA

A. PARKER BURROUGHS

Published by The History Press
Charleston, SC 29403
www.historypress.net

Copyright © 2014 by A. Parker Burroughs
All rights reserved

"A Death in the Lyric" appeared first in serialized form in the *Observer-Reporter*, Washington, Pennsylvania, in 2012.
"The West Enders: A Story of Murder in Desperate Times" appeared first in serialized form in the *Observer-Reporter* in 2013.

First published 2014

Manufactured in the United States

ISBN 978.1.62619.400.7

Library of Congress CIP data applied for.

Notice: The information in this book is true and complete to the best of our knowledge. It is offered without guarantee on the part of the author or The History Press. The author and The History Press disclaim all liability in connection with the use of this book.

All rights reserved. No part of this book may be reproduced or transmitted in any form whatsoever without prior written permission from the publisher except in the case of brief quotations embodied in critical articles and reviews.

For Alice, my wife and best friend

CONTENTS

Preface   9
Acknowledgements   11

1. A Death in the Lyric   13
2. An Unholy Passion: The Tragic Tale of Martin Reed   33
3. "Shreds of Quivering Flesh": The Explosion that
   Rocked Washington   55
4. The West Enders: A Story of Murder in Desperate Times   69
5. The Wreck of the Cannonball Express   99
6. The Murder of Thelma Young   115

Bibliography   137
About the Author   141

PREFACE

Violence came to Western Pennsylvania the moment Europeans stepped on its soil. The French and British fought over it during the French and Indian War. When settlers first arrived and established the Ohio River as the edge of the frontier, they battled the Native Americans. Attacks on forts and farms were followed by bloody reprisals. As if that weren't enough, roving packs of bandits terrorized this lawless land in the later half of the eighteenth century.

Soon after independence, the law arrived. Thomas Richardson, a burglar and member of the notorious Doane gang, was the first to be hanged on Gallows Hill above what is now Washington in October 1784. The violence continued as Washington County grew in population. Twelve more men convicted in the county would be executed for murder in the next century and a half. Those men and the stories of their crimes are now mostly forgotten, along with other calamity that is nevertheless woven into the fabric of local history and culture.

Washington County's most famous crime came on New Year's Eve 1969, when Joseph "Jock" Yablonski; his wife, Margaret; and their daughter, Charlotte, twenty-five, were shot to death in their Washington County home by three assassins. The murders stunned the quiet community of Clarksville, where the reform candidate for the United Mine Workers of America (UMWA) presidency and his family lived. Yablonski's assassination was ordered by W.A. "Tony" Boyle, president of the UMWA.

Preface

The shocking Yablonski murders were the subject of several books. This volume, however, is about crimes that have long since passed from memory.

The six stories in this book have been resurrected from old, brittle news clippings and from the dust-covered volumes of bound newspapers in the archives of the *Observer-Reporter*, descendant of the *Reporter*, founded in 1808. These news reports recorded the events as they happened, in all their confusion and contradiction. The passage of time creates a clearer focus. I have used the news articles as a guide to sift through trial transcripts, government documents, letters and other remembrances and, through forensic journalism, to assemble the facts in narrative fashion.

These are true stories. In a few places, I have imagined details to enhance the flow of the narrative; however, no dialogue has been invented. The characters speak in their own words, as recorded in trial transcripts and other sworn testimony, recollection of witnesses and direct quotations in published articles.

I discovered most of these tales through serendipity, stumbling across them while researching more mundane subjects. Many more stories from Washington County's history—some just as intriguing and disturbing as these—lie dormant in the crumbling pages of the past, just waiting to be told.

ACKNOWLEDGEMENTS

This book would not have been possible without the assistance of a man who died forty-five years ago. Earle Forrest began meticulously to save newspaper clippings soon after he began work at the *Washington Reporter* in 1920 and kept it up for nearly fifty years. The result was a couple of filing cabinets packed with twentieth-century Washington County history. It is from those cabinets that sprang most of the stories in this book.

Those clipping files are the property of the Observer Publishing Co., which has employed me for nearly as long as it did Forrest. I thank my friend, publisher Thomas P. Northrop, for his unflagging support, encouragement and, of course, all those paychecks.

My wife, Alice, was critic, editor and proofreader of these stories.

Among those who assisted me in my research were Clay Kilgore and the staff of the Washington County Historical Society; Ella Hatfield, research librarian at Citizens Library; the staff of the Washington County Clerk of Courts; Sally Scheidt, Barbara Miller and Bob Mish of the *Observer-Reporter*; Fort Vance Historical Society; and employees of the Burgettstown Community Library and Heritage Library, McDonald.

I also wish to thank family members of Dorothy Horne and Ray Kunselman for their help with "The West Enders" and descendants of Sylvester and Iva Young for their assistance with "The Murder of Thelma Young."

1
A DEATH IN THE LYRIC

The ringing telephone awakened James H. Shannon MD in the darkness before dawn. A few minutes later, he was walking swiftly up Main Street, bundled against the near-zero temperature. Snow was falling lightly on the Sunday morning of February 3, 1907. The only noise the doctor would have detected was that of his own footsteps until he had nearly passed the Lyric Theatre and heard a commotion in the alley. He turned and saw several men carrying what appeared to be a body into the doorway of the building at 78 North Main Street. One of the men hailed him, and he followed the group up the stairway and into a room, where they laid their motionless burden on a bed.

One look at the partially clothed young woman told Dr. Shannon she was quite clearly dead. Her face was still frozen in what he knew as "risus sardonicus," literally "mocking laugh." It was not so much the expression of the corpse that startled him, though, but rather the fact that he knew her.

Frances C. Martin was a pretty eighteen-year-old, with brown eyes, brown hair and a fair complexion, sturdily built at five feet, four inches tall and weighing 140 pounds. She had been to young Dr. Shannon's office just three days earlier, when he found her to be in good health but also pregnant.

The Harvard-educated Shannon, at thirty years old, had only recently begun his practice in the borough of Washington, Pennsylvania, after having interned at hospitals in Boston, Massachusetts. He rented a room at the corner of West Prospect and Dewey Avenues and kept an office at 63 South Main Street.

Illustration by Robert Mish.

Frances had been upset by his diagnosis. Shannon would later testify at the coroner's inquest that she told him she planned to kill the man who had done this to her and then kill herself. He testified that he advised her against doing so.

How Frances died, Shannon could not say just yet, but her last moments must have been in terrible agony. He turned his attention from the dead girl

A Death in the Lyric

to the men who had carried her into the room: John T. Innis, twenty-seven, a tin worker who went by the nickname "Spikes"; John V. Cook, stage manager of the Lyric Theatre and into whose apartment the body was taken; and Daniel B. Forrest, thirty-seven, manager of the Lyric and a member of one of Washington's most prominent families. There was something suspicious about their behavior. Why had they taken the girl's body from wherever she died to the Cooks' home? What were they trying to hide?

Shannon would need to fill out a death certificate, but the place where she died was obviously not where the group now stood. What Shannon told them was more accusation than statement of fact. "The girl did not die in this room," he said.

None of the men who had carried her body from where she did die—the room above the box office in the Lyric Theatre—across the alley and into the stage manager's home was a stranger to Frances. She had lived in John and Mary Cook's home, where she was employed as a maid. The Cooks permitted her to go out on Saturday evenings with Innis, her boyfriend of the previous two years. And Innis was good friends with Forrest; they were the only two people who had keys to the bedroom above the box office that would, in the coming weeks, become the focus of civic outrage.

Main Street, Washington, circa 1910. *Illustration by World West Galleries.*

The mystery of Frances Martin's death would be solved quickly, but its effects would reverberate through town for years to come. Moral decay was rotting the foundations of the borough, and the death in the Lyric would bring it all into the light.

Fast Growth and Fast Times

Though it had been laid out a century earlier, Washington was, by 1880, still a sleepy little farming town of 4,292 souls, mainly the descendants of Scots-Irish settlers. But then a large pocket of gas was struck in 1884, an event that would change a village into an industrial city in a single generation. Washington would experience a boom in prosperity and population—and all the problems that come with such growth.

That gas well on the Hess Farm off Jefferson Avenue in Tylerdale was not the first drilled in the area, but it did prove to be the most productive. Within four months, many businesses in town and forty-six residences had gas service. Where gas is found, so is oil. By 1887, more than five hundred oil derricks were counted within the city limits, and production from the Washington field exceeded eighteen thousand barrels a day. The new millionaires built themselves grand houses.

It was the availability of natural gas, along with the huge reserves of coal in the region, that would have a lasting effect on the borough. Gas brought the Hazel-Atlas glass plant here in 1887, followed by Tyler Tube & Pipe in 1890. By 1895, Duncan & Miller, Highland, Phoenix, Novelty and Pittsburgh Window Glass were operating factories here. Findlay Clay Pot and Jessop Steel would follow in 1902.

With the industry came people. By 1890, Washington's population had jumped 65 percent to 7,063. By 1910, it had increased to 18,778, making it the fastest-growing town in Pennsylvania. Part of that increase was due to the incorporation of South, West and North Washington, but the new jobs accounted for most of it.

The region's ironworks were fueled by coal; mining coal was dirty, dangerous and labor-intensive. While American natives and immigrants alike were pouring into Washington to fill jobs in the new factories, coal companies were busy recruiting miners throughout Europe. Washington was suddenly a crowded town where at least half a dozen languages might be heard.

A Death in the Lyric

With the influx of people came crime and disease that offended the Presbyterian sensibilities of borough natives. Prejudice is apparent in local newspaper articles of the day, which were peppered with racial and ethnic slurs. The papers recognized the proper, upstanding townspeople and elevated them above the common rabble. Editorials began to focus on criminal activity and moral decay, but it is clear from news accounts of that day that drunkenness, debauchery, theft and corruption were not confined to immigrant households. Graft and bribery had seeped into politics and the police department, and those upstanding citizens with their newfound fortunes were keeping many a speakeasy and brothel in business.

Washington was a dry borough, officially, in that the sale of alcohol to the public was prohibited. Some private clubs were permitted to serve drinks, and doctors could prescribe alcohol to their patients for purchase at pharmacies. The demand for alcohol grew with the population. Washington had many clubs and twenty-five pharmacies dispensing beer, wine and liquor by prescription from some of the town's forty-four physicians, many of them specializing in the practice.

Gambling was illegal as well, but townspeople didn't have to look far for a poker game. Prostitution was rampant. The *Observer* reported in 1907 that it counted forty brothels, speakeasies and gambling houses in just one ward of the borough.

Washington's residents spent their money on legitimate entertainment, too. The Opera House occupied the top floor of town hall, located where the county courthouse is now and moved in 1899 to Brownson Avenue. The Lyric Theatre, which could accommodate much larger stage productions, opened on North Main Street that same year. It was conceived and erected by W.D. Roberts and brothers Joshua and Robert Forrest, all prominent local businessmen. The Lyric opened in October with *The Highwayman*, a popular musical comedy of the day.

Lavish productions attracted the finest of Washington's citizenry, but less respectable shows also took the stage. Several years into the twentieth century, talk began to circulate about the Lyric Theatre's clientele. Young, attractive women with questionable reputations were rumored to be receiving free tickets and hooking up with seedy male patrons.

Some clergymen began referring to the borough as a cesspool. They preached that beer parties and drugs were luring children away from families. Police claimed they had no legal power to raid illegal establishments, but everyone else claimed the police were paid by the brothel and bar owners to protect them.

The body of Frances Martin was removed to this building at 78 North Main Street, Washington, where she was pronounced dead. *Photo by the author.*

Disgust grew and then gave way to shock when the events of the morning of February 3, 1907, became known. The Lyric—or more specifically, a bedroom above its box office—would capture the community's attention, fascinate and sicken it and, finally, move it to action.

A Death in the Lyric

A Girl in Trouble

On the frigid morning that Frances Martin suffered an agonizing death, her boyfriend, John T. "Spikes" Innis, was arrested and lodged in the county jail. Though the cause was not known at the time, it was obvious to county detective William McCleary that Innis had something to do with her demise. Several witnesses told McCleary they had seen Innis with the young woman throughout the evening, and it was Innis who summoned help and was with her when she died.

Following a coroner's inquest a few days later, Innis would be cleared of involvement in Frances's death, but he would still face other charges that grew out of his testimony at the hearing: aiding in procuring an abortion.

Although he was advised by Coroner William Sipe that he was not compelled to answer questions, Innis was candid. He testified that he had known Frances for four years and had been intimate with her for the past eighteen months. More than a year earlier, in December 1905, when Frances was seventeen years old, she had informed Innis that she was pregnant. Innis said they talked it over and decided on an abortion. Shortly after Christmas that year, he went to Pittsburgh and procured the necessary instruments and drugs for the procedure, which was performed successfully in one of the rooms above the Lyric Theatre.

One year later, about three weeks before she died, Frances told Innis she was pregnant once again. This time, Innis testified, they talked about getting married.

Frances apparently had some doubts about her boyfriend's commitment and sought the advice of a fortuneteller, who told her, "Spikes will never marry you." After this, Frances drafted an agreement—one that she showed to her friends and which was entered as evidence at the inquest. It read, "I hear by [sic] state that on the tenth day of December, in the year 1906, that John T. Innis promised to marry Frances C. Martin after his mother's death, and Frances Martin agreed to this and so did I."

Innis testified that he had heard about the agreement but had never seen or signed it.

Frances had confided in a friend, Carrie Prowitt, that she was considering killing herself if Innis would not marry her. On January 26, Frances went to the McNulty Drugstore at 92 North Main Street and asked the druggist, Frank DeNormandie, for poison to kill a cat that she said "was running about with all the hair off it and about half dead." DeNormandie advised her to drown the creature because strychnine was an awful death, and she left without buying it.

Irene Martin and her two other daughters were living in Indiana, Pennsylvania, at the time of her daughter Frances's death. Mrs. Martin and daughter Elizabeth came to Washington when they were notified of the tragedy. The mother visited Innis in the jail on Monday, February 4, and afterward spoke with reporters. From what she told the press and later testified at the inquest, giving birth to an illegitimate child, or even death, would have been better for Frances than a life with Spikes. The following account of an interview with Mrs. Martin the day after her daughter's death was published in the *Observer*:

> *The story told is a sorrowful one and showed the love of a mother for her child, regardless of what the past life of the girl had been.*
>
> *…Innis had often abused Frances and had said he would choke her to death unless she did as he told her. Mrs. Martin says she has seen Innis choke Frances and has driven him out of the house while a resident of Washington because he insisted on abusing the girl.*

What was the Lyric Theatre became the Washington Theatre in the 1920s. *Courtesy of Observer Publishing Co.*

A Death in the Lyric

At age fifteen, Frances had gone to work at the William H. Griffiths Tinworks, where she met Innis. At that time, her mother and two sisters were living in rented rooms on West Cherry Alley and later above a furniture store on East Wheeling Street, now occupied by Countryside Frame Shop. Her brother had been placed in a reform school. When her mother and sisters moved to Indiana, where they would find work at the new Pennhurst State School and Hospital, Frances became a domestic for John and Mary Cook, next door to the Lyric Theatre.

As "successful" as Frances's abortion was, she lost her job in the Cook household over it. Mrs. Martin managed to convince her daughter to come to Indiana, but she testified at the coroner's inquest that Innis had sent Frances money and persuaded her to return to Washington, where Mrs. Cook agreed to take her in again.

In agreeing to employ the recently disgraced Frances, Mrs. Cook had insisted that she not go out with Innis except on Saturday nights.

About 7:30 p.m. on Saturday, February 2, 1907, Frances told Mrs. Cook as she was preparing to leave for the theater that she would not return that night. She said she expected a final answer from Innis that evening, and if he refused, she would first kill him and then herself. But just before stepping out the door, Frances told Mrs. Cook, "I have thought of a better plan. I will have him arrested Monday."

Frances's Last Date

Mary Cook could hardly believe what Frances Martin had just told her: that instead of killing her boyfriend and then herself, she planned to have him arrested. The wife of the Lyric Theatre's stage manager watched her hired girl walk out the North Main Street apartment and turn toward the theater next door. She would never see Frances alive again.

By 7:30 p.m., the air had turned colder, and a light snow began to fall. At the box office, Frances picked up the ticket that her boyfriend, "Spikes," had left for her—a fifty-cent reserved seat—and walked down the long, narrow hallway past the poolroom to the theater.

The performance on the night of February 2, 1907, was *Sleeping Beauty and the Beast*, a Victorian pantomime. Advertisements for the show announced a company of sixty actors performing in the tradition of London's Drury Lane productions. These were elaborate shows that featured stunning costumes

Daniel Forrest, manager of the Lyric Theatre. *Library and Archives Division, Heinz History Center, Pittsburgh.*

and sets that changed quickly and often and mechanical devices that could rotate and elevate props and backdrops.

Frances was seen to leave her seat and return several times during the performance. One of those times, she headed up the hall, past the box office to the sidewalk and turned right, walking a few doors up the street to McNulty's Drugstore.

At the coroner's inquest a few days later, druggist Frank DeNormandie testified that Frances had entered the shop and told him the cat she wished to be done with was still alive and that she wanted strychnine to kill it. He wrapped the poison in paper and handed it to her without a comment.

In the theater's ladies' parlor after the show, Frances met thirteen-year-old Anna Watson. It's not clear from testimony at the inquiry whether Innis introduced her to Frances or whether Frances met Anna on her own and then introduced the child to Innis. At any rate, Frances invited the girl to go upstairs with her. The two went through the box office, where theater manager Daniel Forrest was sitting at his desk. He acknowledged the pair as they climbed the staircase to the large room at the front of the building.

The room was eighteen by twenty-six feet, with three large windows overlooking Main Street. The furnishings included a bed, couch, dresser and center table and a Brussels carpet. In one corner was a sink with warm and cold water, and the walls were decorated with, as the *Reporter* described, "pictures of an obscene nature such as are usually found in places used for what the room is alleged to have been kept for." The article continued: "It is said by those who have been investigating the case that the room was used almost nightly for immoral purposes and drunken debauches."

The room could be entered through the box office and up a narrow stairway, as Frances and Anna did, or through another door that exited to the main hall of the second floor. In order to get into the main hall, it was necessary to go into the building from Main Street, down the first-floor hall, through the poolroom and up another staircase.

Soon after Frances and the girl entered the room, so did Innis and Amos Martin (no relation to Frances), who was employed by the Lyric as an electrician and was in charge of the poolroom. Amos left to buy four club sandwiches, and Frances and Spikes went down the hall to see about getting

The cover of a program from 1903. *Courtesy of George Simms.*

some beer. While they were gone and Anna was left alone, Forrest came into the room through the box office staircase.

Anna had never been in the room before but had an idea what the night might lead to. She had been living on her own since dropping out of school and leaving her family, getting into all kinds of trouble. It would have been no surprise to her when Forrest came upstairs from the box office, put his arms around her, kissed her and handed her a bottle of beer.

Forrest asked Anna who her company was for the evening and if he might be able to spend some time with her after the show some night.

Innis was in and out of the room all night. He left once to pick up a letter that Frances had written and given to her friend Carrie Prowitt. In the letter, Frances had written that she intended to kill herself if Innis would not marry her. Innis kept his distance from Frances. There was a poker game going on down the hall that went on into the early hours of Sunday, and Innis spent most of his time there, returning to the room at about 1:30 a.m. and again at 4:00 a.m.

Anna would later testify that she spent most of the evening talking with Amos and that the two got into bed together at 3:30 a.m. Which bed or room the couple used was not made clear in the testimony that would follow, nor was it clear whether Frances stayed in the room above the box office all night. But in the early hours of Sunday morning, Anna Watson said she noticed Frances unwrapping a package and putting something in her mouth. Frances said it was medicine but did not elaborate.

At 5:50 a.m., Frances told Anna that she was going to die. About ten minutes later, Innis came back to the room to find Frances in convulsions. He ran through the hall and down the stairs to the poolroom, where Amos was sleeping on one of the tables.

"Oh, God, Frances is dying!" Innis cried before running from the room.

Center of the Cesspool

"Oh, God, Frances is dying!" Spikes kept crying. Amos watched him run from the room. At first he thought Spikes was simply joking. Then, as he got his senses about him, he realized that couldn't be. Amos quickly left the building and ran past Chestnut Street to the Lewis Hotel, where theater manager Daniel Forrest was living. Amos roused him from sleep and told him what Spikes had said.

A Death in the Lyric

"For God's sake, Martin, that cannot be!" he said, and the two hurried back to the theater.

A few minutes later, Forrest and Spikes carried the lifeless body of Frances Martin down the steps and into the alley. At that moment, Alfred Thomas, described in newspaper accounts at the time only as "a colored man," was walking by and was summoned by Forrest to help them carry the body to the building next door. When they reached the door, Forrest told Thomas to leave and warned him not to say a word about what he had seen to anyone.

Forrest's stage manager, John V. Cook, opened the door, and the three began carrying their burden into the building at 78 North Main Street just as Dr. James Shannon approached.

Daniel Forrest was a member of one of Washington's most prominent and respected families. Several of the buildings on Main Street were constructed by his father, Joshua Rhodes Forrest, and his uncle Robert R. Forrest, and a section of North Main was called the "Forrest block."

Joshua Forrest graduated from Washington High School and began studying at Washington & Jefferson College but left at age seventeen to join the Union army during the Civil War. Less than a month after his enlistment, he was with General Ulysses S. Grant at Petersburg. He fought with the army through Virginia in the last days of the Confederacy and was present for the surrender at Appomattox.

Joshua returned home to study law, but eventually his real estate holdings at the time of Washington's great oil boom made him wealthy and occupied his attention. He and his wife had three children: Daniel, born in 1872; Earle, born in 1883; and Alma, born in 1890. Though there is no historical evidence to prove it, Alma was probably not the child of Mr. and Mrs. Joshua Forrest but rather Daniel Forrest's illegitimate daughter, raised as his sister by his parents.

Daniel graduated from Washington & Jefferson College as well and began working for the family businesses; among them was the Lyric, Washington's first theater. In 1890, he married Ella Frye. The marriage did not work, and at the time of the tragic event of February 1907, Daniel found himself living alone in a hotel room.

The grief, or the panic, that young Dr. James Shannon saw on Daniel Forrest's face was not entirely due to the corpse he helped carry upstairs that frigid morning. Forrest's dark demeanor had much more to do with the effect the death would have on attendance at his theater and the damage it would cause to his own reputation and that of his family.

Strychnine rapidly enters the blood, and symptoms of poisoning usually appear within twenty minutes. They begin with cramps and soon culminate in powerful and agonizing convulsions that subside after a minute but recur at a touch, a noise or some other minor stimulus. Victims often experience uncontrollable arching of the neck and back and tightness of the jaw.

Though Dr. Shannon had his suspicions about Frances Martin's death as he examined her that morning, it would take an autopsy to confirm them.

On Monday, February 4, Shannon performed the autopsy. He testified at the coroner's inquest two days later that he had found what he believed to be strychnine in the stomach, along with a small amount of liquid and bread. He said that all of her muscles showed signs that she had taken the poison. The intestines and bladder were greatly contracted, the liver was enlarged and white spots were visible all over the spleen. He concluded that she had died in convulsions.

At a cost of $1.50, the stomach was sent for analysis to a laboratory in Pittsburgh, which confirmed that strychnine was present.

The doctor's testimony at Coroner Sipe's inquest was heard by a jury of six men: John Curran, clothier; Thomas Bebout, farmer; W.P. Wilson, reporter; Lee Knode, a clerk at Gabby's shoe store; William Ecker, reporter; and George Y. Fields, the proprietor of a poolroom. After hearing witnesses in secret most of the day, they returned the following verdict: "We the jury, find that Frances C. Martin came to her death on Sunday morning, February 3, 1907, in a bedroom in the Lyric theatre, from the effects of strychnine, which from the evidence we believed to have been self-administered with suicidal intent."

Though no one would be charged with aiding in Frances's death, the criminal activity it uncovered would be prosecuted. Following the inquest, county detective McCleary arrested Spikes Innis on the charge of aiding an abortion a year earlier. Innis's boss, tin mill owner William Griffiths, posted his $1,000 bond.

On February 7, 1907, the *Reporter* noted:

> *The most sensational feature in connection with the coroner's investigation… was the arrest of Daniel B. Forrest, manager of the Lyric Theatre, who is charged with keeping a bawdy house. Forrest gave bail in the sum of $500 with his father, Joshua Forrest, who owns the theatre building, as surety…*
>
> *The information against Manager Forrest was made by Detective William McCleary at the insistence of District Attorney Underwood.*

A Death in the Lyric

Forrest had been subpoenaed to testify at the coroner's investigation into the death of the Martin girl. As soon as testimony had been adduced to the effect that the girl had died in a room above the box office in the Lyric Theatre and that the room was kept by Manager Forrest, officers were at once sent out to arrest Forrest. The arrest seemed to come as a surprise to Forrest, who grew very pale when the officers placed him under arrest.

There would be hearings for Innis and Forrest two weeks later. Innis was held for court, but charges against Forrest were dismissed for lack of evidence. Though he was cleared of charges in Frances Martin's death, Daniel Forrest's troubles were not over.

In fact, they were just beginning.

A Call to Action

On the Sunday morning that followed the hearing, the Reverend Pressly Thompson, pastor of Second Presbyterian Church, delivered a sermon decrying the moral conditions in Washington. It was a theme repeated in pulpits all over town that day and through the remainder of winter.

The next day, on Monday, February 18, the borough council directed its solicitor to draw up an ordinance giving police the power to raid brothels and speakeasies. Police had claimed that they, unlike constables, lacked the authority to conduct such raids. Many residents believed, however, that police were reluctant to bust establishments they were paid under the table to protect.

A group of church women, to whom the *Observer* referred as "the most respectable women in town," announced a boycott of the Lyric Theatre, calling it a "vicious place and one which should be shunned by all respectable people, both young and old." The women were critical of the Day Nursery association for sponsoring a fundraising presentation of *Cinderella* in the theater a few days earlier. The association said the venue had been booked months earlier, and due to extensive advertising, the location of the performance could not be changed.

The entire town was swept up in a sense of indignation over the activity at the Lyric Theatre and the many other seedy public places that Frances's death had brought to light.

But Joshua Forrest, father of the disgraced manager of the Lyric, was outraged for another reason. Reeling from the damage to his family's reputation, on February 19 he filed suit against the Observer Publishing Company, seeking $10,000 in damages. The suit claimed that the *Observer*, in publishing news of Daniel Forrest's arrest for maintaining a bawdy house, did so "falsely, maliciously, wickedly and illegally."

The following day, an *Observer* editorial, in a veiled reference to the lawsuit, declared:

> *We shall always have wickedness with us in some form or other. Providence perhaps has in its workings, brought this community face to face with the present deplorable state of affairs, the half of which the* Observer *has not told and cannot tell in print. Many of our best citizens are familiar with them. And because they have this knowledge and have acquainted themselves with the situation, they are aroused to the need of concerted action for the betterment of conditions. When the citizens as a whole, of every condition in life, almost unanimously condemn the practices which have been exposed, and urge us to go forward with the work, we would be false in our mission and to the best interests of this community if we did not continue our influence to uproot the evils. We assure our readers and the people of this community that we will continue to expose the evil and to call to the attention of those in authority the prevalence of crime, wherever it may be, and in this we are no respector of persons, whatever the consequences may be...*

In printing this statement, the young newspaper publisher and owner of the *Observer*, John L. Stewart, gave notice to politicians, police, citizens of varying repute and Joshua Forrest himself that the newspaper would champion the cause of community betterment and not be bullied by lawsuits while doing so.

Though there was not enough evidence to try Daniel Forrest initially, testimony at a juvenile hearing for Anna Watson gave pause to the district attorney and provided yet more ammunition for the group of churchwomen promoting the boycott of the Lyric.

Anna, the girl who was with Frances Martin in her final hours, was believed at the time of the inquest to be about sixteen years old. She was actually just thirteen at the time she was propositioned by Daniel Forrest and seduced by Amos Martin in the infamous bedroom above the Lyric Theatre.

The hearing before Judge James Franklin Taylor was held to determine what should be done with the child. "The story told by the father of the girl was a pitiful one and showed how completely the child had been under the influences responsible for the existence of the notorious room over the box office," the *Observer* reported.

He said his daughter had been incorrigible for some time and that he was not able to make her go to school. He said he didn't know her to stay out all night, except when she stayed at the places she was working. He was placing her in the hands of the juvenile court so that it might "get her in an institution where she could receive a proper training."

Judge Taylor asked the probation officer to try to find a suitable home for Anna outside Washington. The girl had objected to going to Morganza and expressed a wish to get out of town so she might be free from her old companions and associations and start a new life. She was later placed in the Rescue Home for Girls in Pittsburgh.

Anna Watson's fateful visit to the room above the theater on the night of February 2, 1907, might well have saved her from a miserable adolescence. Many Washington girls, some as young as Anna, who should have been going to school were instead working in filthy brothels.

The churchwomen, with the help of their preachers' sermons, kept the pressure on the Lyric Theatre and its manager. On March 8, Edith Rick, a renowned Pittsburgh orator accustomed to performing before packed houses, was to make her first appearance in Washington with her monologue, *Hearts and Faces*, which was heavily advertised. By 8:15 p.m., only six patrons had entered the theater. After waiting in vain until 9:00 p.m., manager Daniel Forrest called off the performance and closed the doors. The boycott had been successful.

Washington's council took action later in March, approving fines of not more than fifty dollars or thirty days in jail for those operating gambling dens or brothels. The *Observer* reacted with indignation. The newspaper and many citizens expected the council to ban such places and run the operators out of town.

"Instead of doing this the council has done the very opposite," an editorial on March 20 read. "It has in reality passed a measure of regulation. In other words it might be considered a license to conduct these places upon the payment of $50 every once in a while, the periods being determined by the chief of police…We do not want these places of vice and iniquity regulated. We want them prohibited."

The last word of that editorial would be repeated over and over again in the coming years. More and more people would be won over to the idea of prohibiting the sale and consumption of alcohol. Locally, politicians found support of temperance to be nearly a requirement for office. Prohibition became a popular political movement that would culminate in the ratification of the Eighteenth Amendment in January 1919. In Washington, Frances Martin's death had given a push to this cause.

Weak ordinances or not, Daniel Forrest was practically run out of town. All shows at the Lyric for the remainder of March were canceled, and it was announced that management would be taken over on April 1 by Nixon Zimmerman & Company, which declared that the Lyric "would be all that the best people of the community desired it should be."

Pittsburgh's Samuel Nixon and Fred Zimmerman had teamed up with the New York theatrical production team of Marcus Klaw and A.L. Erlanger to form the Theatrical Syndicate, which in 1907, and for another decade, would monopolize theater bookings throughout the United States. The theater in Washington, soon to be called the Nixon, would get only the shows selected by that syndicate.

Forrest, disgraced and fearful of more charges to be brought against him, left town, never to return. He settled in Kenton, Ohio, where he remarried and entered the retail and wholesale tobacco business. He suffered a stroke in 1916 and another in 1917, which killed him at the age of forty-seven. Though his siblings and parents survived him, only his brother, Earle, showed up for his funeral.

Irene Martin, Frances's mother, wished to have her child's body brought to Indiana, Pennsylvania, for burial, but the expense was too great. John "Spikes" Innis offered to help out and, with the help of his and Frances's former employer W.T. Griffiths, purchased a plot in Washington Cemetery, where Frances lies today, her grave unmarked on a sun-splashed hillside.

Innis would come to rest in the same cemetery twenty-three years later. He had been working as a watchman at the Highland Glass plant when he died on July 20, 1930, at the age of fifty-one. He left a wife, Sarah, and four children.

Washington would not be reformed overnight. Its battle to save its young from sexual promiscuity and disease and from the ravages of drugs and alcohol would go on—a fight still being waged today. But the death in the room above the Lyric Theatre that fateful night brought the town back to reality from its reverie of growth and progress. Evil had moved into the neighborhood.

The Lyric Theatre would live on by other names. After a few years as the Nixon, it became the Globe and, later, the Washington Theatre. It would undergo two major renovations and would end its life as the Penn Theater, falling to the wrecking ball in the mid-1970s as part of the Bassettown redevelopment project.

Where the Lyric once stood is now a city parking lot. The brick wall of 78 North Main Street faces the lot, and on it can be seen where a window and doorways have been bricked over.

It was through one of these portals that the body of Frances Martin was carried in the darkness on that frigid morning so very long ago. Visit that wall by moonlight in the quiet of night, and you might hear young Dr. Shannon's hurrying footsteps padding through the snow and coming around the corner or the hushed whispers of conspirators.

Close your eyes, and you might sense that ancient grief, remorse and panic.

2
AN UNHOLY PASSION

The Tragic Tale of Martin Reed

From the floor of the icehouse where Martin Reed lay, the firing of Springfield rifles sounded like popping corn. The bullets piercing the double-planked walls created a shower of splinters and pinpoints of light in the dusty darkness. Between bursts of gunfire, Reed heard the muffled barking of orders, shouts and taunts of a growing crowd and the furious beating of his own heart.

The sheriff's posse had surrounded his hiding place, and the fugitive Reed, gripping a revolver in each hand, knew there would be no more escaping. We cannot know what raced through this desperate man's mind that hot August afternoon in 1892, but searing memories of the woman he loved and the terrible mistake he made in pursuit of her must have been among them.

How had he gotten himself into such a mess? Where did it all start?

Candor, a sleepy little hamlet in Robinson Township in northern Washington County, is a cluster of houses surrounding a hill on which sits a stalwart church, the brick on its shaded walls darkened by age, a graveyard of ancient, tilting tombstones on its southern side. From this vantage point, farmland stretches to the horizon in every direction—in summer, a vast, rolling quilt of emerald and gold.

The village is little changed from Candor of more than a century ago. Although giant derricks drilling for Marcellus shale gas now come and go from these farm fields and the flaring of new wells often illuminates the night sky, this is not so different from the early 1890s during the area's oil and gas boom. At that time, derricks rose like whiskers from the McDonald field,

Washington County Murder & Mayhem

Raccoon Presbyterian Church, Candor, Pennsylvania. *Photo by the author.*

which by the end of 1890 was producing eighty thousand barrels of crude oil a day.

At that time, the people of Candor and of hundreds of other little villages in Western Pennsylvania were mostly the descendants of the Scots-Irish who settled here on the very edge of the frontier in the late eighteenth century to battle the rocky soil, fickle weather and Native Americans. They worked the land as their hardy forefathers had, raising wheat and corn and grazing cattle. Upper Raccoon Presbyterian Church in Candor was established in 1789, and the present edifice was finished in 1872.

The oil boom made many farmers rich, particularly those lucky enough to own land above the saturated Gordon Sand. Not so the Reed family, whose luck was anything but good.

In the same year the new church was built, John Reed, a church elder and a highly regarded young man, suffered a horrific death. John was on the Nat Pollock farm with family members and neighbors, harvesting wheat by means of a steam-powered Massillon thresher. Straw was the fuel used to fire the boiler of the machine—the forerunner of the combine—on which he was working. A fire began in the straw piled around the machine, and in his attempt to escape, John fell into the grinding cylinder and was trapped. As the fire raged around him, John pleaded with his neighbors. "Chop me out!" he screamed. The crew could do nothing but look on in horror, and when the fire finally subsided, little of the man was left to bury.

We do not know for sure if Martin Reed, then about fourteen years old, witnessed his older brother's death, but given his age and the nature of family farming, it is quite possible that he did. Such a sight would likely have had long-term effects on those who witnessed it, and some of Martin's friends thought the experience may have had something to do with his behavior in his later life.

For his time, Martin Reed was a big man: six feet tall, well over two hundred pounds and exceptionally strong. He also had a weakness for strong drink.

Reed was married in 1880 and brought his seventeen-year-old bride, Annie, to live with him on the family farm in North Star, five miles from Candor and just across the Washington County line in Allegheny County. But only six weeks later, Reed left home, explaining to Annie, "I am not treated well here." He would never spend another night with his wife.

Friction among the Reed siblings became public knowledge when many of older brother Henry Reed's herd of cattle became sick and died. Henry accused Martin of poisoning them and told neighbors that he had found a jar of white powder in a locked box of horse medicine kept by Martin.

Martin's younger sister, Maggie, once had to press charges against her brother for being drunk and causing a disturbance, but she denied rumors that their spring had been poisoned or that the family had to feed their bread to dogs before feeling safe enough to eat it.

At a dance in Candor at Christmas 1888, Agnes, the twenty-three-year-old wife of Alexander Chappel and the mother of his two young children, caught Reed's attention. Reed knew Chappel, who had moved his family into a house on the Robert Geary farm; they were occasional drinking companions, but he had never seen Chappel's wife. Reed and Mrs. Chappel danced together twice that night, and although they probably felt an attraction, they would not lay eyes on each other for another year.

At a Christmas celebration the next year, Chappel asked Reed to come to his house on New Year's Eve for a goose roast. He told Reed that he had a keg of beer hidden in a cave on the property, and he wanted Reed and other friends to help him drain it. The carousing that went on for nearly two days aroused indignation among Candor's more conservative residents.

Reed and Chappel became close. Because he supplied his friend with whiskey, Reed was frequently invited to the Chappel home. One time, in the autumn of 1890, Reed visited the farm to find Chappel away on business. Mrs. Chappel said her husband was expected to return that night and that Reed should wait for him. Chappel did not come home, however, and Reed did not leave. What transpired that night will never be known, and the fact that Aggie Chappel gave birth to her third child about nine months later might have been coincidental.

In May 1891, Reed was working on the Geary farm and moved into the Chappel house as a paying boarder. The two men were still close friends at that point, but soon Chappel became suspicious, as did the gossips of Candor. Chappel began to wonder if the child in his wife's womb was his. Normally gregarious, his demeanor changed; he became sullen, seldom spoke and was prone to explosions of rage.

When his wife went into labor in July, Chappel at first refused to send for the doctor. He eventually did leave to find Dr. Donaldson, but when he did not return and the birth became imminent, Reed went and found another doctor and told him he would pay the bill.

A McDonald woman, Mrs. Hight, had come to the house to assist Mrs. Chappel with the birth. She would testify later that Reed came into the bedroom shortly after the delivery with some whiskey and wine and implored Mrs. Chappel to drink something. Reed had his elbows on the bed and had nearly crawled into it, she said. Mrs. Chappel took a little wine, and Reed said, "If Mrs. Hight tells about this, we'll murder her, won't we, Ag?"

Later that summer, Reed suffered a gash on his head in a farming accident. He might have recovered quickly had not erysipelas, a severe strep infection, set in. Dr. Hill thought the infection would kill him. Reed's wife, who had since moved to the village of Midway, pleaded with Reed to return home with her so that she could nurse him back to health. When he recovered, he could go where he wished, she said.

Reed declined. "I will stay with Aggie if she'll have me, or I will go to a hospital," Reed said, according to several witnesses.

During Reed's recovery, Chappel grew more agitated and told his wife that people were talking and that he wanted Reed to leave.

When he was strong enough to be on his feet, Reed asked the doctor if he was well enough to travel to Pittsburgh. The doctor said he could, so long as he stayed away from liquor. On Monday, October 5, 1891, Reed went to Pittsburgh for an unknown reason and returned with two bottles of whiskey. Reed offered one of the bottles to Mrs. Chappel so that she might give a little to settle a cranky child. Four months later, she would be shown that bottle again and asked to identify it before a hushed crowd in a Washington courtroom.

So Long at the Fair

On the morning of Thursday, October 8, 1891, Alex Chappel and Charley Geary, the adopted son of the farm's owner, started out for the Burgettstown Fair in a horse-drawn cart. They saw Reed and asked if he wanted to go along. He declined but said he might come later.

At about 10:00 a.m., Reed mounted his horse, a strawberry roan with four white feet, and started off for the fair, six miles away. He noticed his mount had a strong cough.

The Burgettstown Fair had been held every year since the 1840s. Historian Alvin Dinsmore White, in his *Historical Sketches of Northern Washington County*, wrote that the United Agricultural Association, which organized such country fairs, forbade the sale and use of alcohol on the grounds, as well as pool selling or betting on speed. White continued:

The Burgettstown rail depot during the annual fair. *Courtesy of Fort Vance Historical Society.*

However, a few thirsty people were able to evade the rules with impunity by secretly carrying their own flasks from which they would be able to take a sly swig in the privacy of one of the many horse stalls on the fairgrounds. Such thirsty ones were aided also by a few well-known and easily recognized "boot-leggers" who managed to get onto the grounds with an ample supply of the contraband. One of these was said to have been a well-built woman whose garments were so well supplied with pockets in which she carried the wet goods that she could scarcely walk when she first arrived on the grounds.

Geary said they encountered Reed on three or four occasions as they strolled the fairgrounds that day, and Reed asked them several times when they planned to return home and by which route. Reed met them late in the afternoon, when they were getting ready to depart, and asked Chappel if he was thirsty. Reed then pointed to a fencepost and said that he had seen two men drink from a bottle of whiskey and hide it there. Chappel went to look for it but couldn't find it, so Reed pointed it out to him. Chappel thanked him and offered to go somewhere and drink with him, but Reed said that his horse had a bad cold. He said he wanted to walk it home and had better get started.

Too many people were around for Chappel to drink in the open, so he slipped into the stable of Hood's Hotel. He found two men in there—Stewart

Floral Hall at the Burgettstown Fair. *Courtesy of Fort Vance Historical Society.*

Liggett and George Harris—whom he didn't know, but he offered them a drink. Each took a sip and then watched as Chappel downed the rest of the bottle. Chappel returned to the cart where Geary was waiting, and the two headed out the road toward Candor.

"Give me a slug of tobacco," Chappel said to Geary. "That whiskey had a bad taste. I think it was Jamaica ginger."

At about 5:00 p.m., Dr. Nesbitt was summoned to a room in Hood's Hotel, where he found Harris violently ill. "At the least touch he would be convulsed, the muscles contracting with such force that he could not be held," Nesbitt would later testify.

Meanwhile, just half a mile from Burgettstown, Chappel, who had been complaining to Geary about a severe stomachache and had asked Geary to slow the cart, screamed out in pain and tumbled into the road.

Walter Porter, who was milking his cows nearby, heard Geary's cries for help and came running to find Chappel prone and twisted on the road, his face contorted and blood trickling from his mouth. Geary then went running back to town for help. Another farmer, William Ross, arrived to assist Porter. Chappel "had a clicking sensation in his throat. He was so convulsed we had to lift the whole body to place a blanket beneath his head," Ross would later testify.

Geary returned with Dr. Nesbitt just in time to witness Alex Chappel's death.

It was after seven o'clock when Martin Reed arrived at the farm in Candor, and Robert Geary asked him where his son Charley and Chappel were. Reed said he was surprised they had not passed him on the road home and suggested that Chappel was probably drunk.

Two hours later, Charley Geary returned in an excited state and, finding Reed, pulled him aside and told him that Chappel was dead.

"Is that so?" Reed replied.

Geary was taken aback by Reed's lack of surprise. He explained the manner of the man's death.

"You'll have to go back to Burgettstown and identify the two men who hid the bottle," Geary said.

Reed said that there was no use for him to go and that he would not do so. Reed did, however, offer to inform Mrs. Chappel about the death of her husband.

Murder Most Foul

Although the two men in the stable who had sipped from Chappel's bottle were gravely ill on the Thursday night of the fair, within a few days both had improved to the point that doctors were confident of their survival. The cause of their illness was strychnine poisoning. This was confirmed by results of tests in a Pittsburgh laboratory on Chappel's stomach, which had been removed during an autopsy, placed in a jar and sent to the city by train.

Charley Geary was summoned to the coroner's inquest in Burgettstown on Saturday morning, October 10, and pointed out the post where the bottle Chappel took had been hidden. He also testified that Reed's horse had been tied to the same post earlier Thursday. Hoof prints were still visible in the earth around the post. Those prints indicated an unusual plate shoe that matched those of Reed's horse. Based on this evidence and the fact that no one else had seen the two men who supposedly hid the bottle and no one else had been sickened, Reed was charged with the death of Alexander Chappel and the assault on the other two men. He was taken to Washington County Jail to await trial.

In earlier years, Reed's trial might have commenced in a few weeks, but cases were backing up in Washington County Court, and Reed would have to wait four months before facing a jury of his peers. The discovery of gas and oil brought an influx of industry and wealth to the community. Bountiful coal resources were exploited to fire the furnaces of the iron and steel mills, and along with this came a surge in population and crime. Murder—foul and unusual as it once was—had become commonplace; the court was awash in cases. But Chappel's murder was different. It would attract great attention, not because of its means, but because of its motive.

As District Attorney William Saunders Parker would summarize in the opening argument of Martin Reed's trial: "We will show that the defendant, two or three months before, became an intimate of the Chappel home, that there crept into his heart and life an unholy passion, which the history of the world shows to be the case of more crime than any other."

The trial began on Monday, February 15, 1892. The jury of twelve men included eight farmers, a teacher, a blacksmith, a merchant and a "gentleman." Judge John A. McIlvaine, District Attorney Parker and defense attorney Martin L.A. McCracken were among the elite of the Washington County legal community. McIlvaine, in his fifth year on the bench, would retain his seat for thirty-five years, retiring at age eighty-two in 1922. McCracken was the judge's former law partner. Parker was the acknowledged leader of the

An Unholy Passion

The old courthouse was demolished in 1898. On the left is town hall; on the right is the sheriff's residence. *Courtesy of Observer Publishing Co.*

county Republican Party, of which both McIlvaine and McCracken were stalwart members.

Tuesday's proceedings began late, at 10:00 a.m., due to a landslide on the Chartiers Railway that delayed the arrival of some of the witnesses.

It was not until Wednesday's session that the motive behind the poisoning was explored in any depth. Robert Geary, the owner of the farm where the Chappel house was located, testified that Chappel was deeply troubled in the weeks before his death and that Reed had told him that Chappel was not the father of Mrs. Chappel's last child. The elder Geary said he had known Reed all his life. He said that on the fateful night Reed returned from the fair, he showed no surprise that Chappel had died and asked no questions. He also said that when a neighbor, Todd McCutcheon, came to the Chappel house to view the body, Reed told him, "I haven't seen him yet, myself, and I don't like to look at him."

The large crowd in Judge John A. McIlvaine's courtroom became attentively hushed when the victim's widow, Agnes Chappel, took the stand as a prosecution witness. Under the questioning of District Attorney Parker, Mrs. Chappel admitted that Reed, just after her third child was born but before his head injury, had asked her to leave her husband and to go away with him. Parker then read several letters from Reed to Mrs. Chappel, one of which began, "Oh, my dear Aggie." Parker read another letter that Reed had written to her from jail asking her to write to him often and to take care of his horse. The horse was Reed's only possession, and he said that she should have it. "Do you blame me for poisoning Alex?" Reed wrote. He went on to say that the couple had always treated him well, he had never had words with either Aggie or Alex and Alex had never done anything for which he should punish him.

Parker called her attention to the whiskey bottle, to which Reed was alleged to have later added the poison that killed her husband, and she said it was the same bottle Reed had brought back from Pittsburgh; the same bottle from which she took some alcohol to soothe her child.

Under cross-examination by Reed's attorney, Mrs. Chappel denied that she and Reed were ever "criminally intimate."

Reed took the stand in his own defense late Wednesday and was still testifying on Thursday morning. Displaying an air of seriousness and extreme confidence, he denied being responsible for the death of his brother's cattle and said the only poison he'd ever used was to kill ground squirrels. He said that there had never been any trouble between Alex Chappel and him and that he had never had intimate relations with Mrs. Chappel. He swore that his only intention in writing her letters was to inform her of how and when he would pay his rent.

The day concluded with a 150-minute closing argument by Reed's attorney. The *Observer*'s account stated that McCracken "went over the evidence, commenting on it from the defendant's point of view, making mole-hills out of the mountains of which were in Martin Reed's path to freedom."

On Saturday morning, District Attorney Parker, suffering from a cold, addressed the jury for nearly three hours, his voice growing so hoarse that he ended his lecture in nearly a whisper. After Judge McIlvaine's charge to the jury, the panel adjourned to deliberate at 2:10 p.m.

As the hours rolled by, several of Reed's friends bade him goodnight, but Reed was so confident of his acquittal that he told them, "Wait till the jury comes back and I'll go with you." The jury, however, did not return on Friday night. After seven ballots, one juror was still insisting that Reed was not guilty.

The jury did return with its verdict on Saturday morning, grimly filing into a packed courtroom. To many, the announcement by foreman Samuel Rankin, a South Strabane Township farmer, was unnecessary. The grave faces of the jurymen had already told their decision.

Judge John A. McIlvaine. *From* Biographical Record of Washington County, Pa.

According to the *Observer*, Reed "took it with characteristic impassibility, the only show of emotion being the cold perspiration that sprang from his brow."

Sentencing was deferred until Monday morning, February 22, in order that a motion for a new trial by Reed's attorney could be heard. At that time, Judge McIlvaine said the reasons for a new trial were insufficient, and the motion was refused. The condemned man was then sentenced to be hanged by the neck until dead.

Reed, who had protested his innocence throughout, stood motionless throughout the sentencing, his eyes wandering from the floor to the judge and back. At the judge's last words, he dropped into his chair. A moment later, Deputy Sheriff John Kennedy tapped him on the shoulder, and he arose to go back to the jail. As the reporter for the *Observer* wrote, "He left with a firm step, then broke down and cried like a baby for his mother."

A Time to Plot

Life and the rapid pace of change went on, and readers of the local newspapers moved on from the Reed trial to other news, some of it trivial, some of it titillating. On the day Reed was sentenced, a young man from

Greene County by the name of Mr. Kiger was reported to have appeared at the telegraph office at the Baltimore & Ohio rail station in Washington in an alarmed state. The man explained that he and his bride, after being married in Ohio, were en route to Waynesburg, but along the way, they had lost their marriage license. He feared that without proof of their legal union, their reputations would be ruined. A search for the document was reported to be underway.

The market for coal was exploding, and readers learned that Norway was interested in acquiring Pennsylvania coal because English coal had become too expensive. That the economy had already become global was evident in the fact that shovels manufactured in Charleroi were then being shipped by way of the Monongahela, Ohio and Mississippi Rivers to South American ports and the Sandwich Islands.

Sexual assaults were frequent and reported in the newspapers in much detail. The suspect was typically a "notorious colored man," the victims always churchgoing young women of impeccable virtue. The May 19 issue of the *Observer* reported that Miss Hattie Van Eman and her sister Annie were assaulted on their way from a prayer meeting by David Burgess, who was said to have tugged at one of their skirts. Burgess was taken to await trial at the county jail, where Martin Reed was still incarcerated and waiting for his execution.

While his attorney took action to postpone the hanging, Reed grew restive in the aged jail. Because of the nature of his crime, he was placed in a cell by himself, while other inmates, like Burgess, most confined for petty crimes, were held in a cell housing as many as forty inmates or permitted to roam the interior of the jail. But Reed was determined not to end his life at the end of a rope. In the months of his imprisonment, his friends and even his wife, Annie, had visited him, and concealed in their clothing were items Reed intended to use to escape: saws, files and even guns.

On the evening of Thursday, May 19, 1892, court was in session for the arson trial of Hugh Curry, accused of setting haystacks afire in Amwell Township. The trial had attracted wide interest, and people from all over the county had come to Washington to witness it. One of those spectators was J.B. Schaffer, an oil driller from New Castle, Pennsylvania. He was a Civil War veteran who had served as a color bearer in the Eleventh Pennsylvania's Reserves.

Meanwhile, inmates were in a raucous mood, making a great deal of noise. Five of them, however, had convened beside Reed's cell and were seen to be talking with him in conspiratorial whispers. They were

An Unholy Passion

Fred Cottham, a German immigrant held for theft; Joe Brown and Fred Smith, gamblers; Ted O'Neil, a burglar; and George Evans, jailed for selling illicit whiskey.

Just after sunset, the group of five managed to pry a door off one of the cells and used it as a lever to attack Reed's cell door. They pulled apart the bars enough to create a space of about twelve inches by twenty-four inches. Even as large as he was, weighing about 230 pounds at the time, Reed was able to squeeze through. The men then went to work with a pump handle on an exterior wall of the jail. The old brick and mortar crumbled easily, and in a matter of minutes, they had punched their way through.

The hole was twenty feet above the ground outside. A rope made from torn blankets was lowered, and Brown shimmied down and scurried across the yard into the darkness. Reed, with two revolvers tucked into his belt, turned to the watching prisoners and warned them that he would shoot and kill anyone who tried to prevent his escape, with the exception of Deputy Sheriff John Kennedy.

At eight o'clock, Schaffer left the courtroom and went into the yard to get a drink from the pump. As he was doing so, he watched as Cottham came out of the hole and climbed down the makeshift rope, which broke in half, sending Cottham tumbling to the ground the last ten feet.

"What are you doing?" yelled Shaffer.

Cottham got to his feet and sprinted in the direction of West Beau Street. Shaffer then ran around to the jail entrance to alert the guards. As he was doing that, Reed came down what was left of the makeshift rope, jumped the rest of the way and fled into the night.

Shaffer alerted one of the sheriff's deputies, who ran into

This engraving of Martin Reed was distributed with his description and notice of a $500 reward for his capture. *Washington Observer.*

the main area of the jail and ordered O'Neil, Smith and Evans to come away from the hole in the wall or be shot. They would learn later, much to their chagrin, that the deputy had been unarmed.

The commotion moved the crowd from the Curry trial to the front of the jail, where they raised a hearty cheer when Sheriff William P. Cherry mounted his horse and, as the crowd assumed, galloped off in pursuit of the fugitives. But Cherry stopped his mount just a few paces away at a Main Street drugstore, from which he emerged with a fistful of cigars. He jumped back in the saddle and whipped his horse up Main Street to a second round of applause interspersed with hooting and laughter.

Deputies and borough police fanned out over the town but found no trace of the escapees. Supposedly, they had been seen along the Middletown Road (now Route 844), and searchers concentrated in that direction.

Police later heard that Brown and Reed had been spotted in the Wheeling, West Virginia rail yard at about 4:00 a.m. on Friday but could not confirm the report.

Washington County's commissioners immediately sent telegrams to surrounding towns and cities, and a circular with an engraving of Reed's image was mailed to all postmasters and chiefs of police. The circular described Reed as being "well built, erect bearing, large round face, heavy dark mustache, short dark hair, scar on top of head, front, near the middle, large prominent dark gray eyes of striking expression, wears No. 9 shoe." He was also described as wearing a dark sack coat, dark trousers with narrow stripes and a soft hat.

The board of commissioners offered a $500 reward for Reed's capture, dead or alive. Commissioner W.S. Bailey was confidant Reed would be captured shortly because "he has none too bright an intellect and is destitute of friends."

After Fred Cottham fell from the broken blanket rope, he sprinted down West Beau Street, then turned south on Franklin and made his way to the B&O trestle. He walked from there past the station and up the tracks heading northeast. Rain had begun to fall shortly after the escape, and by the time he reached Finleyville, he was soaked to the bone. He then jumped a freight train, getting off at the B&O roundhouse in Glenwood, near Pittsburgh, where he was arrested Friday morning.

Cottham's capture was welcome news, but it was just a stroke of luck, as all effort was going toward finding Reed and bringing him to justice. Washington Police chief John A. Orr and county detective William McBride were embarrassed and incensed by the jailbreak and swore they would not rest until Reed was once again behind bars.

An Unholy Passion

At 3:30 a.m. on Friday morning, just seven and a half hours after the inmates broke to freedom, Orr and McBride pounded on a door of a house in the village of Midway, where Reed's estranged wife, Annie, had been living for a number of years. They knew she had visited her husband just a few days earlier. They informed her of the jailbreak, and she displayed no surprise.

Neither Orr nor McBride was of the same opinion of Reed's character as Commissioner Bailey. Reed might have been a brute, but he was not stupid, and it was quite obvious from the turnout at the trial and from the number of visitors at the county jail that he had more than enough friends, some of them willing to take great risks to keep him free.

Their early morning visit to Midway was the beginning of an arduous, four-month search of farms and villages in northern Washington County, where McBride believed Reed was hiding. They would come close to catching him on a number of occasions, only to be frustrated by the fugitive's knowledge of the land and uncanny sense of danger. But their relentless determination would eventually be rewarded.

Wealth and Stealth in the Oilfields

Washington Countians had for years complained about the inadequacy of their jail, but the escape by Reed and his associates was the impetus needed to convince both elected officials and taxpayers that a new one should be built.

In its May 23, 1892 edition, published four days after the escape, an editorial in the *Observer* expressed a most common opinion:

> *With no more formidable battering ram than a pump handle, the rotten brick wall is pierced and justice is in a fair way to miscarry. The imperative need of the hour is a new jail, built in connection with a new courthouse commensurate to the wealth of this great county. Our neighboring counties of Butler and Fayette, neither of which are equal in wealth to Washington, have within the past few years erected magnificent structures. Why should Washington lag in the rear? As a matter of fact the present building is as unsafe a repository for official documents as the jail is for prisoners. The title deeds to many of the fairest estates in the county could crumble to ashes should a fire occur. The litigation resulting would be endless, the loss, irreparable.*

Several years earlier, some local politicians had proposed constructing a new courthouse by issuing ten-year bonds and raising taxes by a mere rate of one mill. That was before vast revenue from the gas and oil boom swelled the county coffers. By the time Reed's escape heightened the need for a new prison, the new money made a much more ambitious project possible.

By October 1891, Washington and Greene Counties had become the most productive oil-producing area in the nation, with fifty thousand barrels a day pumped from the McDonald field alone. By November, the output would soar to eighty thousand barrels a day.

Where oil was not found, gas was, and the reliable source of it brought heavy industry, particularly glass manufacturing, to Washington. Along with the industry came people—lots more of them. The sudden growth in population was accompanied by a sharp increase in crime. In the same week that Martin Reed was arrested, two murders in McDonald, both brutal slayings of women, garnered little attention. Such activity in the boomtowns of the oilfields was becoming common.

Just six years after Reed's escape, the county embarked on an immense project to upgrade its facilities. Town hall, a massive brick structure, was moved from Main Street about 150 yards to Cherry Alley and Brownson Avenue to make way for a new jail and a courthouse that would put any other county to shame. The new buildings opened in 1900.

A few days after Reed's escape, Detective McBride teamed with Midway constable Samuel Williamson to scour the territory where Beaver, Allegheny and Washington Counties meet in search of their fugitive. With Sheriff Cherry covering their expenses, the pair followed leads and for eight weeks came tantalizingly close to their prey, who seemed always a few steps ahead of them.

According to what McBride would later tell the *Reporter*, Reed first went to Arden and hid there in an old mill for three days. On the Monday following his escape, he was spotted near Midway and later at a coal bank near Candor, where he stayed until June 2. Williamson had searched there that night, striking matches in the dark and coming within twenty feet of the fugitive, Reed later told one of the people who harbored him.

On Saturday, July 23, the pair received a tip that Reed was working on the Scott farm in Mechanicsburg, Beaver County. When they arrived there, they asked Mrs. Scott who was the man who was working there. She said it was her nephew but refused to give his name. While they talked at the front door, a man broke from the rear of the farmhouse and ran toward a thick forest known as the Wilderness. McBride fired three times at him, but by that time, the fleeing man was out of range.

An Unholy Passion

McBride sent word to Cherry to come with a posse. A number of men, including Washington's Chief Orr, arrived and searched the woods—to no avail. Orr remained tracking his prey along Raccoon Creek and eventually to a brother's farm in North Star. Orr told the *Reporter*:

> *From there we believe he went straight to Peter Wackers's place at Noblestown and has since remained in the buildings about the slaughterhouse. Wackers and Martin have been great friends, Peter being a butcher and peddler and well known throughout all the country. On Friday (August 5) we learned that he was at Wackers's concealed about the slaughterhouse buildings somewhere. We reached there about 1 p.m. Saturday and McBride tried to get some men in the town to help reconnoiter among these buildings. They just guyed him, however, not believing that Reed was about at all. A little before two o'clock we decided to investigate this ice house.*

Reed's Final Stand

Wackers's slaughterhouse was at the upper edge of the village of Noblestown, just a couple miles from the Washington County line. The icehouse, a wooden structure, twenty by forty feet with twelve-foot walls, stood a little apart from the other buildings in a hollow beside a small run. In the still, sweltering heat of that afternoon of Saturday, August 6, 1892, the only sounds the lawmen—Orr, Williamson and McBride—heard were the babbling brook and the buzzing of flies.

The icehouse had a door at the side of one end and a gable with an opening closed off by a wooden door. The trio quietly approached. Williamson and McBride took up positions outside, and Orr entered the building carrying his Winchester rifle.

"Just to the left of the door was a large ice chest, ten feet high, and a partition from this to the wall cut off a space of about eight feet square," Orr later told the *Reporter*.

> *In this partition was a door, fair in front of the outside door. This was fastened on the inside, but I kicked it open. The whole inside was in plain view, and was empty, except two chairs. The only place a man could be was on the ice chest. I got my rifle in position and started to back across*

> the room. When about half way across, a man suddenly raised up on the box and fired.
>
> I recognized him as Reed. He had a most diabolical look on his face. His beard was full grown, perhaps an inch and a half long, and his hair uncared for and straggling in every direction.

The next thing Orr saw was the flash from Reed's revolver. The bullet entered Orr's left arm, which had been raised to hold his rifle. It exited his shoulder and then reentered his back, where it lodged. Unable to hold up the gun, Orr walked out of the building and yelled, "He hit me! But it's only a scratch."

The lawmen then looked up to see Reed, who seemed to be trying to get out of the icehouse through the gable.

"Come down and surrender!" McBride shouted. According to the report published the following day in the *Pittsburgh Dispatch*, "Reed ripped out an oath and slammed the window shut."

The gunshot and the shouting could be heard in the village, and soon a crowd began surrounding the icehouse. Peter Wackers arrived, went to the outer door and opened it. Orr ordered him to shut it and then, he said, feeling weak, "I went to Dr. Taylor's office and had him bandage my arm, and sent a telephone message to Sheriff Cherry, and sent to Oakdale for Springfield rifles belonging to Company C."

By the time Orr returned, the mob had grown to about one thousand townspeople, many of them still laughing at the idea of Reed being in the building. Many men in the crowd had come armed with handguns, hoping for a chance to shoot the fugitive should he run out of the icehouse.

Policemen, sheriff's deputies and constables began arriving to help with the capture. One of them arriving on the train from McDonald with rifles supplied by Colonel Nesbitt of the National Guard was Hugh Coyle, a sheriff's deputy who had been acting as a cop in McDonald.

By the time Coyle arrived at Wackers's place at 5:00 p.m., there had been no noise or sign from Reed for two hours. During that time, hundreds of rounds had been fired at the building to little effect.

Coyle marched up to the icehouse and announced that he was going in.

"Don't go in. He will kill you," Orr said.

"By God, I will go in anyway," Coyle said. "I want that reward."

Coyle entered the outer door, and just as he entered the inner doorway, Reed fired a shot and missed his mark. Coyle jumped out the door and hollered, "We've got you now! You might as well come out!"

Coyle plunged back into the building, and just as he opened the inner door, another shot rang out.

"I stood fair in front of the two doors and saw Reed shoot, Orr later recounted. "Coyle turned round and came out laughing. He stepped to the corner and then for the first time reached for his revolver. Just then he swayed over in front of the door, whirled round, staggered and fell among some weeds about fifteen feet from the building." Dr. Taylor, seeing that the bullet had pierced his heart, declared him dead.

"The crowd seemed possessed of fury, and longed for the life of Reed as a tiger longs for its prey," wrote the reporter for the *Pittsburgh Dispatch*.

McBride, Orr and Williamson were at a loss for what to do next when they were approached by Richard Singleton, an oil well shooter, who had an idea. With the lawmen's permission, Singleton placed five quarts of nitroglycerin against the wall at one of the corners of the building with the intention of blowing a hole in the wall large enough to get a shot at their target. Although the explosion was deafening and sent a shock wave through the crowd, it accomplished little more than creating a hole in the earth.

It was now after 6:00 p.m., and the crowd was growing impatient. The lawmen worried that darkness could make it possible for Reed to escape, but they were more fearful of the mob and what violence it might create.

"Set it on fire!" some people in the crowd around the icehouse screamed. "Burn him out!"

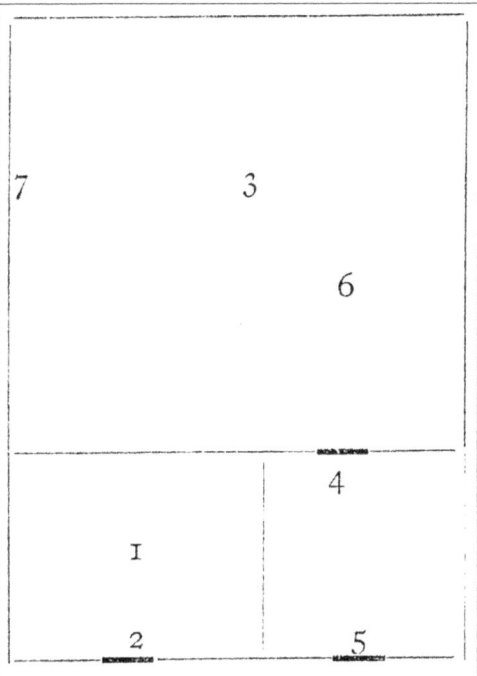

1—Ice chest on which Reed lay when he shot Orr. 2—Window in gable through which he thought to escape. 3—Orr's position when shot. 4—Door in which Coyle met the fatal bullet. 5—Outside door. 6—Where Reed stood when he shot Coyle. 7—Where Reed's body was found.

A diagram of the icehouse in Noblestown. *Washington Reporter.*

When Sam Norcross brought a bucket of oil and a ball of packing material to the side of the building, the men who had worked tirelessly for the last eleven weeks to capture Martin Reed and take him back to Washington, preferably alive, to face the punishment ordered by the court stood by, powerless to stop what would happen next.

As flames began to lick the side of the icehouse, a great cheer arose from the crowd. The *Pittsburgh Dispatch* reported, "It was but after a few minutes when nearly all the old frame structure was wrapped in fire, where the smoke rolled backward to the eastward and a cast of curling, ghastly shadow hung over the valley."

Scores of men stood along the hillside with their guns raised, waiting for a chance to shoot the fleeing man. From the agitated audience, someone shouted he had seen Reed in the window. Some claimed to have heard a scream. Then, above the roar of the flames, three distinct gunshots were heard. A moment later came a crackling of perhaps one hundred explosions as fire reached Reed's cartridges.

When the boards on one side of the building were burned through, a burning body could be seen lying beside the opposite wall. Men rushed forward and hastily tore off the boards. The body was pulled out of the heat using a long hook fashioned from a gas pipe. The corpse was badly burned and the face charred beyond recognition.

The body was removed to the depot, where word came from Washington County coroner McDowell to send it to Pittsburgh on the midnight train. Williamson accompanied the remains to the city, where a funeral director judged the cause of death to be a gunshot to the heart. The body was placed in a crude wooden coffin, which Williamson escorted back to Washington, arriving at the B&O station at 5:27 p.m. on Sunday. From there, the coffin was moved by wagon to the sheriff's office behind the courthouse, followed by a large crowd of men and boys. As soon as the wagon passed into the courthouse yard, the iron gates were closed to keep the curious at bay.

Once inside the sheriff's office, the lid of the box was removed, releasing an odor of burnt flesh. The corpse lay on a bed of excelsior, wrapped in a sheet. The *Reporter* published the following description:

> *Measurements taken showed the man to be a very large one. It is stated that Reed when recently measured tipped the beam at 230 pounds. An examination of the body showed that it had been in a fiery furnace. The flesh was burned to a crisp in many places, in some instances the charred bones being exposed to view. The left leg was burned off at the knee. A*

portion of the right foot as well as both hands were gone, their stumps only remaining; they were drawn up against the ankle and wrists respectively. The top of the head was burnt off. An erroneous statement had been made that Reed shot himself in the head, the only shot was one directly through the center of the heart and lung.

Sympathy for the Damned

Washington Police chief John Orr endured a painful operation to remove the bullet that had lodged deep beneath the flesh of his back. By the morning of Monday, August 8, he was feeling "as comfortable as could be expected under the circumstances," and he agreed to be interviewed by a writer for the *Reporter*. Orr gave full credit to the energetic Will McBride for cornering their man and capturing the body. Whether McBride ever received the $500 reward, however, is not known.

Although the men of law enforcement did not experience the satisfaction of seeing Martin Reed hang for his crime, that Reed had been killed at least brought to an end the long and embarrassing freedom the convicted man had enjoyed. Moreover, they had no doubt of Reed's guilt or of the moral necessity to remove him from among the living.

Reed's friends and relatives, and the public in general, were of a different state of mind. Many who knew Reed doubted he was capable of murder and that he was as innocent as he had always proclaimed. Others might have accepted his guilt but thought Alex Chappel deserved to die. For them, the love they imagined to be shared by Reed and Aggie Chappel justified the crime.

Reed received much assistance on his eleven-week flight from the law, and during this time, he became something of a folk hero for his defiance of authority. That summer of 1892, when Reed was on the run, was also the time of the Homestead Strike, when the Amalgamated Association of Iron and Steel Workers waged bloody battle against Pinkerton guards hired by the Carnegie Steel Company. In some minds, Reed's plight and that of the oppressed millworkers were the same and their violent defense noble.

In addition to those who doubted that Reed was guilty and those who thought he had committed the crime but maintained that he did not deserve to die for it, at least one person believed that the body dragged from the burning icehouse in Noblestown was not Reed's at all.

John R. Thomas, a McDonald resident who was in Noblestown on August 6, 1892, and was among the crowd that had gathered to watch the grim spectacle, was convinced that the man who died in the icehouse might have been a criminal, but he was not Martin Reed. Thomas told others in the crowd that day that he had known Reed all his life. He saw the man who opened the window in the gable, and he was not Reed. Thomas said that the man did not swear an oath at Orr, McBride and Williamson but rather begged God to save him.

After the corpse was dragged from the burning building, Thomas retrieved a revolver and said it was the same gun he had sold for ten dollars to a man named Charles Buckheit.

Thomas's claims were ignored by the authorities and the press. Most Washington Countians felt certain that Martin Reed had met his end, including his family, his mother, his sister Maggie and his brother Henry, who buried his remains in the cemetery of the Raccoon Presbyterian Church on Wednesday, August 10.

Still, the fact that the body so badly burned in the deliberate fire was unrecognizable left lingering doubt in some minds. Might Reed still be on the loose somewhere? That was too unlikely a scenario for most people to accept. They would rather think that Martin Reed, in his final moments, when he knew death was near, decided to end his life by stopping his heart with a bullet.

It was that heart and the passion within it that had put him there, the heart that beat so fast the moment he laid eyes on Aggie Chappel for the first time.

3
"SHREDS OF QUIVERING FLESH"

The Explosion that Rocked Washington

In the first rays of light of a cool summer morning, a platform spring wagon with a canvas top pulled by two horses twisted through the streets of the village of Mt. Morris, Pennsylvania. Samuel Bigley snapped the reins, and the team broke into a smooth trot as it entered the Waynesburg road.

Bigley was thirty-seven years old, with dark hair, a dark mustache and a cigar clenched in his teeth. He was wearing a bowler hat and light brown suit, with a watch and chain tucked into his vest pocket. Beside him sat his wife, and on the bench behind them were their nine-year-old daughter and another girl, a neighbor about eleven years old who had been invited to join them on their journey, which would take them through Waynesburg in the late morning of Thursday, July 16, 1891, and on to Washington at the end of the day.

The Bigleys were originally from Bradford, in north-central Pennsylvania, where Sam had started out in the oil business. He had become proficient in the infant industry's most dangerous skill: well shooting. He was the one who loaded the incredibly explosive nitroglycerin into metal cylinders called torpedoes, sending them down deep shafts to blast and fracture sluggish wells and make the oil flow. He had a reputation as a fearless expert but also one with a casual attitude toward safety. Bigley had come to southwestern Pennsylvania when oil and gas were found in the Washington field, and then the family followed the oil boom south into Greene County, eventually settling in Mt. Morris, just a mile or so north of the Mason-Dixon line and West Virginia.

The work as an independent shooter was plentiful and the money good, and Bigley had a thick billfold at his hip and a pocketful of silver dollars to prove it.

The purpose of the journey for Bigley was business; he intended to pick up one hundred quarts of nitroglycerin to use in shooting wells in the Mt. Morris area. His wife and the girls were coming along to visit the stores and attractions in Washington, which was growing quickly, fueled by cash from the energy boom. Bigley would return to Mt. Morris with his volatile cargo, while his wife had decided to take the girls on a much easier trip by way of the narrow-gauge train back to Waynesburg. Twenty-four hours later, Mrs. Bigley would learn how wise a choice that was.

By early evening, the wagon had reached the National Pike and turned west down Pancake Hill toward Washington. The horses' hooves clattered on the hard, macadam surface of the road known as Maiden Street in the borough. Evidence of the oil boom was apparent in the new houses and those under construction on both sides of the street, which now had wooden sidewalks, as they approached town. The tracks of the Baltimore & Ohio Railroad were just a short distance to their right.

Passing by the buildings of the Washington Female Seminary, they continued on Maiden Street until Bigley steered the team north onto Main Street. Mrs. Bigley and the girls climbed down from the wagon when they reached the Hotel Main, across the street from the courthouse. Then Bigley turned right on Beau Street and guided his horses into the R.T. Hallam Livery barn, where they would be boarded for the night.

The Bigleys were given two rooms by hotel clerk J.C. Burson, who had known the family since the time they first arrived in Washington from Bradford.

The hotel was built in 1836 and was known first as the American House. Henry Fulton purchased it in 1846 and renamed it the Fulton House. John and Moses Little purchased it after the Civil War, added a fourth floor and mansard roof made entirely of wood and again renamed it Hotel Main. Widely regarded as a firetrap in the 1890s, it burned to the ground on January 6, 1899, taking half a block of other buildings with it in Washington's most spectacular fire up to that time.

The hotel was a regular watering hole for oilmen during those boom years, and it was know as the most popular "loafing place" for Washington & Jefferson College students and townsfolk.

That evening, John Fair, a shooter for the Acme Torpedo Company who had known and worked with Bigley for the past ten years, met his colleague there and arranged to sell him nitroglycerin that he had stored

"Shreds of Quivering Flesh"

in a magazine (a special area for storage of gunpowder or explosives) on a farm east of town. Bigley was disappointed because Fair told him all he could spare were twenty quarts, and Bigley had counted on acquiring much more. But the two agreed to meet at the farm the next morning and complete the transaction.

Although nothing was recorded in the local papers about what Mrs. Bigley and the girls did that evening, other than purchasing some toys, it is quite likely that they attended a performance of *The Fairies Carnival* at the Opera House, which occupied the top floor of town hall, just south and across the street from the Hotel Main. The show, dazzling under calcium lights, featured a choir of 135 local children.

Friday morning, July 17, was bright and clear and sixty-five degrees when Mr. and Mrs. Bigley retrieved the rig from the livery and headed out East Beau Street to pick up the nitroglycerin, leaving the girls in their room and in Burson's care.

The explosive was stored in a bunker built into a hillside on the farm off the road to Manifold (now Cameron Road in South Strabane Township). Fair would later tell a correspondent for the *Reporter*, "On Friday morning I accompanied Mr. Bigley to the William Barre farm on which the magazine is located and gave him just twenty quarts of glycerin. The cans that it was in did not look very good so we placed it in new cans and were very careful that the stoppers were put in securely."

Nitroglycerin was invented in 1846. It is made by mixing nitric acid, sulfuric acid and glycerin and then separating the resulting nitroglycerin from the acid with water. Under the right conditions, it can be a benign substance that has other uses, particularly as heart medication.

The Bigleys then rode back toward town. Bigley turned his horses off Beau Street onto South College Street, and his wife stepped down from the wagon at the corner of South College and East Maiden Streets, intending to walk back to the hotel, retrieve her daughter and her friend and take them to the Waynesburg & Washington Railroad station in time to catch the 9:20 a.m. train to Waynesburg.

As she bid goodbye to her husband, she hadn't any idea that she would never see him again.

Bigley, puffing away on a cigar, turned his horses east and headed up Maiden Street at a moderate trot. Snuggled into a bed of straw between the benches, secured by ropes and covered with oil cloth and a beaver blanket, were the three cans containing the twenty quarts of nitroglycerin. A box of dynamite Bigley had purchased earlier that morning rested by his feet.

A crowd gathers around the hole created by the nitroglycerin explosion in Washington, Pennsylvania, on July 17, 1891. *Courtesy of Observer Publishing Co.*

"Shreds of Quivering Flesh"

At 8:30 a.m., the borough had awakened, and shopkeepers were just beginning to set out their goods beneath their storefront awnings. Workmen were busy laying the last of the bricks to the new DeNormandie building on the west side of South Main Street as Mrs. Bigley turned the corner and headed up Main toward the hotel.

She might have passed Lee Minton, head clerk at the Margerum boot and shoe store, who had stopped to talk with a friend on his way to his home on East Maiden Street. Minton had built the Queen Anne–style house three years earlier for $2,500 and was working hard to pay off the debt.

J.B Charlton and his mother were in a buggy following Bigley. They were on their way to see a carpenter, Mark Keeney, who lived on the East End of town. Mrs. Workman Hughes Sr. was in the kitchen of the large brick home on East Maiden that she shared with her husband. Her five-year-old granddaughter, Ina, was playing on the front porch.

At 8:35 a.m., a minute after Charlton's buggy had trotted by him, Bigley's wagon passed Minton's House and was nearly in front of the Hughes residence—at what is now 560 East Maiden Street—when the awful calamity occurred.

A reporter for the *Observer*, who had been standing in front of the Female Seminary on Lincoln Street, less than a mile away, wrote:

> *The first thing that was seen was a tall swirling column of yellow dust rising like a water spout into the air, and this was followed almost instantly by a deafening report. Such a noise had never been heard in this place, and the great hills taking up the sound echoed and re-echoed the report as mighty thunder. The great column of smoke as it did, on reaching a height of 100 or 200 feet, spread out over the entire heavens, and soon a mist of flying splinters filled the clear morning air…A great cloud of dust hung angrily over the spot for a moment and then came an awful stillness broken by the shrill whistles of locomotives.*

S.B. Post was mowing a field of hay in East Finley Township, eight miles away, when the concussion from the blast jarred the seat of the mower and startled the horses so much that he had difficulty keeping them from bolting. In Canonsburg, heads of people strolling along Central Avenue turned simultaneously in the direction of the ominous blast.

Mrs. Bigley was in front of Henry Hull's shoe store, just one building south of the Hotel Main, when she felt the terrible shock.

"My God, my husband has been killed!" witnesses heard her exclaim.

"Shreds of Quivering Flesh"

The explosion destroyed the East Maiden Street houses owned by the Hughes family (left) and Minton family. *Courtesy of Observer Publishing Co.*

Little Ina Hughes, seated in a rocking chair on the porch of her grandparents' home not more than fifty feet from the explosion, was later found in the side yard under the rocker, miraculously alive with only a few cuts and bruises. Her grandmother was in the kitchen at the rear of the house when the explosion knocked her down. She ran into the backyard, where a beehive had been toppled, and the angry bees attacked the woman, stinging her numerously about the head, arms and face, so much so that it would take her several days to recover.

Sadie Frazee, walking by a house one hundred yards away, was struck in the head by a piece of the wagon, an injury from which she also would recover.

Where Bigley, his wagon and horses had existed a moment earlier was now a hole in the hard limestone road four feet deep and six feet across. The disemboweled carcasses of the animals lay one hundred feet away; no trace of Bigley would be found immediately.

Oddly enough, although the Hughes and Minton houses were destroyed and twenty-eight others damaged, no one else was injured. Charlton and his mother, who had passed Bigley a moment earlier, were badly shaken but unhurt. James Wheeler and his son, William, were driving to town and were twenty-five yards from the Bigley wagon when the explosion occurred. They were knocked from their seats, and both of their horses were thrown back on their haunches, but somehow they were not struck by debris.

When the dust cleared and the curious began to assemble, it was noticed that the force of the blast had imbedded a horseshoe from one of the animals in the siding of Jacob Holder's house, across the street and fifty yards distant.

Yards were littered with lifeless chickens, killed by the concussion. English sparrows had tumbled dead from the sky.

Bell Telephone Company supervisor J.A. Price was at the Chartiers station on South Main Street, waiting to catch the train to Pittsburgh, when he heard the blast coming from the direction of his neighborhood, where houses were beginning to be hooked up to natural gas lines. A gas explosion, he thought.

"I ran at a 1:40 gait and knocked down half a dozen people on my way out, running to my house in the old creamery building," Price told a reporter later. He found his daughter sitting on the parlor floor; doors, glass and furniture had fallen all around her. "No one in the family was hurt, but not a piece of chinaware in the house remained unbroken."

Windows were shattered as far as four miles away.

Carpenter David Vester had just finished papering his house and rehanging all of his pictures when the explosion knocked them all off the walls, and flying glass shredded his wallpaper.

Telegraph poles were broken and their wires scattered. Trees for some distance were left leafless.

Although the shells of the Hughes and Minton houses were left standing, nearly everything inside them was destroyed—every window and piece of

Boys sit by the carcass of one of the two horses killed. *Courtesy of Observer Publishing Co.*

"Shreds of Quivering Flesh"

furniture broken, every door unhinged. Scarcely a piece of plaster remained on the walls.

It would be several hours before what could be found of Samuel Bigley was gathered in a peck basket and brought to the office of Washington County coroner T.R.H. Johnson, who had hastily summoned a jury for an inquest. The Saturday, July 18 edition of the *Reporter* was precise in its grisly description of the contents, gathered from as far as 150 yards from the crater. "Among the parts found were two pieces of scalp, with the ear attached to one, two pieces of jaw with teeth, some of the flesh of the neck being attached to one piece, a part of the backbone, a piece of rib, a finger and the tongue with that part of the lip with the moustache."

The top line of the story's tombstone headline (one with several descending lines, each smaller in point size than the one above it) was equally gruesome: "Shreds of Quivering Flesh."

Coroner Johnson arrived quickly at the scene of the accident, and it became apparent that his investigation would be jeopardized by the hundreds of townspeople eagerly scouring the area for souvenirs of the disaster. He immediately impanelled a jury of six men, who viewed the destruction, interviewed witnesses and then adjourned until 2:00 p.m., when the group met in the grand jury room of the courthouse. There they viewed the remains and heard testimony from employees of the Hallam stable and from experts about the cause of the explosion.

John Fair, Bigley's friend and fellow well shooter, said it was likely that ashes from Bigley's cigar had ignited the straw in the wagon and thus caused the dynamite to explode first and then the nitroglycerin. He told the jury that Bigley drank some but was not drunk on Friday morning. Thomas Morrissey concurred but also suggested that nitroglycerin leaking from the cans might have dripped onto the springs of the wagon, causing the blast. Fair believed that was not possible.

The jury found that there was no evidence of any negligence on the part of any person that in any way contributed to Bigley's death.

Photographers, both amateur and professional, flocked to the scene. The newspapers, particularly the morning *Observer* and the afternoon *Reporter*, which at that time were in fierce competition, had a field day. Their headlines were oversized and sensational. The 1:00 p.m. edition of the *Reporter* on July 17 began: "Terribly Scattered. The Remains of Sam. J. Bigley Strewn over Large Area. A Small Quantity of Bones and Flesh Gathered Up and Taken to Waynesburg for Interment…"

TERRIBLY SCATTERED.

THE REMAINS OF SAM. J. BIGLEY STREWN OVER A LARGE AREA.

A Small Quantity of Bones and Flesh Gathered Up and Taken to Waynesburg for Interment—Damage to Property Aggregating $10,000 to $15,000—View of the Scene, Embracing the Hughes and Minton Residences—Verdict of the Coroner's Jury—Additional Particulars.

Residence of Work Hughes, Sr. **Residence of Lee Minton.**
Scene of the Explosion.

The above illustration of the scene of the explosion is made from a photograph taken about 10 a. m., Friday, by a representative of the REPORTER with a Hawkeye camera, from a point on the bank on the north side of the B. & O. Railroad track, about 150 feet distant from the two houses. The cut from which the illustration is printed was made in Washington by Fred Christman and Lis Huggins, two enterprising young men who have recently purchased an outfit for this kind of work, and from their quarters in the third story of the Boyle building are turning out as good engravings as can be obtained in the city. Christman & Huggins deserve the hearty support of the business men of Washington who use this kind of work.

Local newspapers were proud of the graphic illustrations they were able to produce. *Washington Reporter.*

"Shreds of Quivering Flesh"

In 1891, no photos appeared in newspapers here. The first successful half-tone reproduction of a photograph in any newspaper had been accomplished only eleven years earlier. To illustrate important events, engravers had to reinterpret photos—essentially, make line drawings based on the photos on metal plates. The *Reporter* editors were so proud of accomplishing this that they boasted about it in the accompanying illustration, which was

> *made from a photograph taken about 10 a.m. Friday, by a representative of* The Reporter *with a Hawkeye camera, from a point on the bank of the north side of the B&O Railroad track, about 150 feet distant from the two houses. The cut from which the illustration is printed was made in Washington by Fred Christman and Lis Huggins, two enterprising young men who have recently purchased an outfit for this kind of work, and from their quarters in the third story of the Boyle building are turning out as good engravings as can be obtained in the city.*

Mrs. Bigley was distraught but not without help in her grief. She had encountered a friend from Greene County the previous night, Minnie McCauley, who would be of great assistance in getting the family back home and the remains of her friend's husband to Waynesburg.

When they met on Thursday night, Miss McCauley arranged to ride back to Waynesburg on the wagon with Bigley, but later Mrs. Bigley persuaded her to instead travel with them on the train.

Although rain fell all day on Saturday, July 18, people from all over the county came to view the destruction. Lee Minton's wife, who had been visiting relatives in Westmoreland County, returned to see her home in ruins, their yard trampled by ghoulish souvenir hunters.

The outpouring of sympathy and generosity was nearly immediate. George B. Martin began a subscription campaign to help the Minton family and was pleased to report many contributions of $10 and $20—a good deal of money in those days. By 10:00 p.m. on Sunday, oilmen at the European Hotel had raised $130 for support of Bigley's family.

With this assistance, what remained of Samuel Bigley was buried in Green Mount Cemetery in Waynesburg. But what happened to Mrs. Bigley and her three children is a mystery. Many in Mt. Morris assumed that the family returned to Bradford, or perhaps to Wilkes-Barre, where Mrs. Bigley's people were from, but years later, relatives there were unable to locate them and initiated inquiries that reached Washington. In 1928, Dr. C.A. Skelton of Dallas, Texas, visited the offices of the *Observer* searching for a clue that might lead to the whereabouts of Mrs. Bigley and her children.

They were never found.

The horseshoe imbedded in the side of a house fifteen feet from the ground attracted great attention. Dr. Homer C. Clark lived near that house and was sure that someone would remove it as a keepsake. He decided he would be that person, and on the night after the accident, he placed a ladder beside the house, removed the shoe and put another one in its place.

Over the years, shoes were removed and replaced several times, but the original remained with Clark until years later, when he presented it to the Washington County Historical Society, which now displays it in the LeMoyne House along with a piece of a wheel hub from the wagon.

Ina Hughes, the child in the rocking chair who miraculously escaped serious injury, later became Mrs. Bruce Wallace of Enon Valley, Lawrence County. In 1937, at a Hughes family reunion in New Castle, she recounted her story and displayed the torn dress she was wearing that fateful day forty-six years earlier.

The Washington County Historical Society possesses a horseshoe that had been imbedded in the side of a house by the blast and a part of a wheel hub. *Photo by the author.*

"Shreds of Quivering Flesh"

Lee Minton, whose debt was eased by generous Washington residents, displayed in the windows of Margerum's shoe store some of the torturously twisted pieces of metal found in his yard. What remained of the Minton house was demolished, and the couple moved to a house on West Chestnut Street.

Only the first floor of the Workman Hughes house, built in 1880 at a cost of $5,000, could be saved. The second floor and roof were rebuilt at an estimated cost of $4,000, and the family continued to live there for many years. The house is still there.

Many examples of the force of the explosion were cited, but John Charlton discovered perhaps the oddest one when he visited the scene of the blast the following day. On the National Pike about three hundred yards from the crater, Charlton found a silver dollar that he surmised came from Bigley's pocket. The *Observer* reported, "It had undoubtedly been lying with the face of the Goddess of Liberty against the reverse side of another dollar. The force of the concussion left the impression of an eagle on it. In other words, the dollar had an eagle on both sides."

The explosion of nitroglycerin on July 17, 1891, was not the first in Washington County, nor was it the last. On May 10, 1910, Frank McCullough, an oil well shooter from Burgettstown but lately living in Steubenville, Ohio, was blown to smithereens when a magazine located in a cave three-fourths of a mile from Burgettstown ignited. Parts of the wagon he had taken there were found a mile away.

And on March 11, 1926, fifty-five quarts of nitroglycerin in a magazine in the woods on the R.D. Wylie farm on Hill Church Road exploded. No one was injured, and the cause was never known.

The event on East Maiden Street in 1891, however, at the height of Washington's oil excitement, with all its drama and oddity and gory detail, will never be forgotten.

4
THE WEST ENDERS

A Story of Murder in Desperate Times

A light but steady rain fell on the city of Washington, Pennsylvania, on the evening of Monday, October 21, 1935.

The State Theater on North Main Street had been showing the romantic comedy *Shipmates Forever*, starring Dick Powell and Ruby Keeler. A few people emerged tentatively from below the marquee, raised umbrellas and turned up the collars of their coats before stepping into the wet chill of the night.

On South Franklin Street, family members gathered around the deathbed of Wray Zelt, a Spanish-American War veteran, bank director and civic leader.

On West Maiden Street at the YWCA, the Community Theater cast was rehearsing *The Late Christopher Bean*, which would open the following Thursday.

In the parlors of bankers' stately homes and the kitchens of glass and steel mill workers all through this gritty factory town, radios were tuned to WJAS for its broadcast of the Wayne King Orchestra.

And in Catfish Alley in Washington's West End, three figures hiding in the partial shelter of a basement stairwell waited silently, smoking cigarettes in cupped hands, the rain pelting the broad brims of their hats.

Sounds were amplified in the damp air. Every time the door opened at Tucker's beer garden on McCarrell Avenue across from the schoolhouse, the three men could hear voices and laughter and the clinking of bottles.

At 9:40 p.m., above the hiss of rain, the trio heard footsteps coming down the alley from Canton Avenue. Fingers slipped into coats and wrapped around pistol grips. A dim silhouette appeared—that of a man, walking haltingly, as warily as a deer, pausing to listen.

Washington patrolman James Armour. *Courtesy of Washington Police Department.*

In the cellar stairwell, motor patrolman James Armour, a twelve-year veteran on the police force, felt the back of a hand tap his thigh and, hearing a whisper, "Now!" bolted up the steps, blasted a beam from his searchlight on his target and yelled, "Put your hands up, Ray!" County detective Frank Creps and state police sergeant William Hanna sprang from their hiding place toward the figure, frozen in sudden illumination.

"Put your hands up! Put them up or I'll shoot you now!" Creps yelled.

The fugitive Ray Kunselman stood motionless, grimacing against the light, his filthy hands at shoulder height. An old gray hat, limp from the rain, sagged low about his ears and eyebrows. He wore a long, tan coat—like the ones worn by service station attendants—and beneath it another coat, a heavy yellow shirt and two pairs of pants. He stood in a pair of four-buckle rubber boots. In the pocket of his ragged coat was a loaded .32-caliber revolver.

Kunselman had acquired the gun from a friend during the more than four months he had been in hiding, and he vowed to use it rather than be captured. But this was no longer the swaggering tough guy his friends had known, the dapper little man with the big temper they feared. Thin and unshaven, with dark circles below his eyes, Kunselman looked far older than his thirty-seven years. And now he seemed nearly relieved to surrender.

Since the morning of June 13, when the body of Dorothy Virginia Horne, nineteen years old, was found along a lonely road in Buffalo Township, Armour had been searching for her accused killer. He knew Kunselman; they were about the same age, and both lived on Fayette Street in the

THE WEST ENDERS

Ray Kunselman was captured in Catfish Alley in Washington's West End. *Photo by the author.*

West End. But they were different people. While Armour joined the police force, Kunselman had gone to work for his father, building oil rigs, and he had gotten into some trouble in his early twenties when he was caught burglarizing Sprowls Hardware in Claysville. Kunselman seemed to have straightened out, though, married and had a couple of kids. But then he abandoned them and began trolling for girls in his father's big Hupmobile. He became a fixture at West End beer joints—respected as a great friend by many, despised as a braggart and a drunk by a few. By early 1935, his drinking and strange behavior began to worry his father and sister.

Armour had been obsessed with capturing Kunselman. He would hear rumors that the fugitive was back in town, but he always seemed to be a few steps behind him. Armour had always believed Kunselman's friends were helping him. They knew he was desperate and were afraid not to help him, afraid that informing on him would earn them—like Dorothy—a bullet in the brain.

When he was off duty that summer and early autumn, Armour would dress in plain clothes, sometimes in disguise, and patrol the seedy bars and grim eateries of the city's West End. He roamed the streets, alleys and back lots in moonlight in pursuit of what at times seemed like a ghost.

It would come out later, at the trial, that although Kunselman had traveled as a tramp, riding trains through Pennsylvania, Ohio, New York and Michigan, most of his time was spent close to home. He had broken into the Eighth Ward School—just a few steps from where he was captured—and used it as his hideaway for most of the summer.

Glassworkers at Washington's Duncan & Miller factory, circa 1935. *Courtesy of Observer Publishing Co.*

The West Enders

And now all the hard work had paid off. Armour had hunches before and had talked Creps and Hanna into what they called wild goose chases. But this time he had him, a shivering animal in handcuffs, sandwiched between his trench-coated colleagues in the back of his patrol car, bound for a jail cell and, Armour hoped, the electric chair.

Now all they'd have to hunt for was the proof that Ray Kunselman had murdered his teenage mistress.

Life Among the Desperate

Although the Great Depression had crushed the nation's economy, smoke still spewed from the stacks of steel mills and glass factories of Washington, Pennsylvania. Orders had diminished, but there was still a demand for bottles, jars and pipe and sheet metal. Millwork was hard and the pay low, but those fortunate enough to have factory jobs and those who mined the coal that fired the furnaces eked out livings and provided for family members who could not.

In the spring of 1935, money was tight, Lewis Fuller remembers. He was born in the house at 403 Addison Street in the city's West End in 1923 and has lived there all his life.

"There were five hundred, well, I don't know about five hundred, but there were a hell of a lot of grocery stores in the West End then. Everybody seemed to have one. Nobody made much money at it—just enough to live by."

His grandparents operated Fuller's Grocery Store, as did his parents. And when he returned from service in Africa in World War II and was denied his job back at Jessop Steel, he went into the family grocery business as well. The store closed for good in 1964.

"The West End was pretty rough back then," Fuller said from his room at the Washington County Health Center. It got worse the farther out—west—you went, but that end of Addison Street was a pretty nice place to live."

The West End was heavily populated, with houses packed tightly together, because it was within walking distance to the factories where many folks worked. Automobiles—and the gasoline to power them—were out of most people's price range.

Margaret McClenathan Townsend had a much more difficult commute. The Penn Commercial graduate found a job working as a secretary for the McIlvaine & Williams law firm. The nineteen-year-old would walk from her farm in Amwell Township to VanKirk Station and, she hoped, catch a six-mile ride into town with one of the residents.

"I earned a dollar a day then, and we worked six days a week," Mrs. Townsend said about a month before her death in 2013.

A dollar a day bought much more in 1935 than it does today. Two days' pay could buy you a decent pair of shoes. In advertisements in the *Reporter*, clothing stores offered underwear for thirteen cents, and markets were selling two pounds of hamburger for twenty-nine cents. But so many who had no jobs could afford none of it. They fell into miserable poverty, and the government had no safety net to catch them.

President Franklin D. Roosevelt did not sign the Social Security Act until August 14, 1935, and regular monthly payments didn't begin until January 1940.

The desperate sought help from relatives, if they had them, and from churches and charitable organizations. Some had no other choice but to beg.

"My mother was on assistance, but assistance was different then," said Joseph Horne, who was born in 1930. "Now, you get a check. Then, you went to where the old Washington High School was, there on Beau Street, and you got potatoes, onions, peanut butter."

The Depression hit Horne's mother particularly hard. Iva Rafferty and Wilbur Horne were teenagers when they married. Wilbur found work as a skating instructor at the roller rink on West Beau Street. He lost his fight with alcoholism in 1932 and left his wife with eight children and another on the way. Without a husband or any income, she and her family were destitute. Her oldest son, Francis, left for the Poe Valley CCC Camp near Williamsport, where he would work alongside other young men building the dam and roads that would become Poe Valley State Park. Two of her daughters, Virginia and Laura, were placed in St. Paul's Roman Catholic Orphan Asylum in Pittsburgh. She moved into a four-room house at 55 Wayne Street with her five youngest children and her oldest daughter, Dorothy, who worked at the Tygart Valley Glass factory.

Though her pay was hardly enough to support the family, Dorothy was invaluable to her mother in helping to keep house and raise her younger brothers and sisters.

We cannot know what was in Dorothy's heart and mind then; we can only imagine the hopelessness that she faced: watching other girls her age going off to high school while she headed for the factory; knowing that she was her family's sole support; realizing that her widowed mother would receive no other help from anyone but her and that she could never, like her brother Francis, leave this place.

In the late spring of 1934, just after her eighteenth birthday, Dorothy Horne met Ray Kunselman. He was not the type of man she expected to be attracted to. He was twice her age and nearly an inch shorter, but he was a charmer, a dapper man in clean, pressed clothing with a neatly trimmed mustache and piercing blue eyes.

And he had money, or so she assumed, because she often had seen him driving a long, gray Hupmobile sedan, and he lived in a big house on Fayette Street.

Dorothy didn't hesitate when Ray asked her out the first time, even though she had heard that he had a couple kids and a wife from whom he had been separated for several years but not divorced. It was exciting to be away from her crowded, dreary house, even if all it turned out to be was sitting in a cracked vinyl booth in a smoky beer garden.

Ray bought her drinks and sandwiches and flashed her around like a piece of new jewelry. He teased her and flattered her, and for the first time, Dorothy felt like an adult.

Dorothy met new people—older people—like Katherine Wilkinson and her husband, Raymond, and very quickly another world, another door, opened for her, and she walked into it without so much as a glance over her shoulder.

What she saw through that door and ahead of her was opportunity, in part for her widowed mother and siblings but mainly for herself.

Ray Kunselman offered Dorothy a way out, but neither she nor he—or anyone else who knew them—could imagine how tragic that escape would be.

Love, in Black and Blue

It was 10:30 p.m. on a Friday in March 1935. A door to the Eighth Ward Athletic Club—more commonly called Tucker's beer garden—swung open, and yellow light splashed onto the sidewalk along McCarrell Avenue.

John Plott, a glassworker at the Duncan & Miller factory, walked in and glanced around. It was usually crowded on Fridays, but on this night, only a few people were there—his buddies Val Tucker and Ernie Sickle and Ray Kunselman standing at the bar. Plott was used to seeing Kunselman with his girl—that young kid Dorothy—and some other couples sitting in the red vinyl booths under a blue cloud of cigarette smoke and a dozen empty beer bottles on the table in front of them. He stepped up to the bar next to Kunselman and asked John Tucker, the owner, for a bottle.

"So, how come you're here alone tonight, Ray?" Plott asked. "Where's your sweetie tonight?"

Ray chuckled and, scraping at the label on his bottle with his thumbnail, said, "She's probably out with someone else."

They talked a little about the news: the looming miners' strike, comedians Laurel and Hardy splitting up and Lefty Grove likely leading the Boston Red Sox to the pennant. But Ray was still thinking about her. "My girl, Dorothy Horne, has no business treating me the way she does, as good as I have been to her," he said.

Ray took a long pull on his beer, turned to Plott and said, "She is going to monkey around until I kill her."

Plott offered a nervous laugh and excused himself to go to the toilet. When he returned, Ray had gone out the door and was standing on the sidewalk. Plott returned to the bar and called John Tucker to come over. Plott leaned over the bar and said quietly to the barkeeper, "Let me tell you what Ray Kunselman just said to me."

Many of his friends must have wondered what was going on in Ray Kunselman's head. He had changed, and that made them wary. Just a few years earlier, he had been a man with a future, with a wife and two kids and steady work building oilrigs. His father was an oilman and had more money than most folks in Washington's West End.

Maybe it was the panic that men face at midlife that made Ray take up with a woman—no, just a teenager—young enough to be his daughter.

Soon after they began dating, Ray became possessive. He was jealous of everyone else with whom Dorothy spent her free time. He and Dorothy would go

Dorothy Horne. *Courtesy of Donna Hertig.*

out frequently with his friends Ray and Katherine Wilkinson. Katherine and Dorothy hit it off quickly, and Ray resented the time they spent together, especially when the two went out to bars and sat with other men.

Ray would come calling for Dorothy at the little house on Wayne Street, just over the city line in Canton Township. He would be driving the 1928 Hupmobile sedan owned by his father, D. Elmer Kunselman, whose initials were painted on the two front doors.

Joseph Horne, one of Dorothy's young brothers, was just five years old in 1935, but he recalls Kunselman's car: "I remember a big car pulling up in the alley behind the Wayne Street house. It seemed like it was two blocks long. I remember talking to Dorothy—she was in the car with him."

Joe, a retired steelworker and U.S. Navy veteran who also tended bar at Pickle's for thirty-one years, spent most of his life in the West End. He had a twin sister, Cecilia, who is deceased, along with all of Iva's children, except Joe and daughter Blanche, who lives in a nursing home.

"The neighborhood was better then. We used to leave the doors unlocked, windows open, no screens, nobody ever was bothered," Joe said.

Nevertheless, early in that fateful year, trouble intruded on the Horne home.

It is an evening in early January, and Ray Kunselman has come calling at the Horne household. Dorothy is sitting at the kitchen table, and he sees that she is wearing new stockings and asks her where she got them. She tells him they were a gift from her mother, Iva.

He tells her she is a liar, that another man gave her those stockings, and he pushes her to the floor and rips the stockings off. Dorothy is crying and kicks wildly with her bare feet, striking Ray in the jaw. He punches her in the mouth.

Hearing the commotion, Iva comes into the kitchen. Seeing Dorothy on the floor and bleeding, she grabs a poker and starts after Ray, but he takes it away from her and pummels her about the face and neck with his fists.

Dorothy, no longer working at the Tygart Valley glass factory, finds work in late March as a maid for Earl and Margaret Engel. She lives in their home at 119 Woodland Avenue in Tylerdale, but the job lasts only two weeks. Iva refuses to let Ray enter her house.

Now it is April, and Dorothy has moved back home. Iva comes in at 4:00 p.m. to find Ray's Hupmobile parked in the alley. Ever since the day Ray attacked her, Iva had forbidden him to enter the house, and he had not. He would instead pull up in the alley and honk the horn for Dorothy. She had heard her daughter and Ray arguing in the alley the night before, again about Dorothy running around with other men, and as she enters the house, she realizes he has defied her and dreads what might come next.

Iva stands at the door and listens to Ray pleading with Dorothy to make up.

"I don't want to make up," Dorothy says. "We're through."

"I will be back tonight," Ray says as he brushes by Iva on his way out the door.

At 9:30 p.m., Ray returns. Iva comes to the door, and it is obvious he has been drinking.

"Is Dorothy home?" Ray asks.

"No, no, she doesn't want to talk to you," Iva says.

Ray pushes past her and into the kitchen.

"Dorothy, get your coat on, I want you to come with me."

"I don't want to go."

"Well, you are going," he says.

"She doesn't have to go with you if she doesn't want to," Iva interjects.

"Well, I'll show you she does," Ray says.

He and Dorothy argue some more. Ray paces about the kitchen, his hands thrust in his pockets, his voice growing louder.

"Ray, what have you got in your pocket?" Iva asks.

Ray lunges at Iva and thrusts something hard in his pocket against her side.

"There is what I've got!" Ray says menacingly.

"Well, Mother, I will go with him," Dorothy says as she slips on her shoes and reaches for her coat.

They can hear the younger children crying in the other room. Iva's face hardens with rage.

"If any of you make any outcry, I will shoot you all," Ray says, grabbing Dorothy by the elbow and pulling her toward the door.

Dorothy's Final Days

The crowd that had gathered at Mike Lombardo's Napoli Spaghetti House on West Chestnut Street to listen to the radio broadcast of the Pirates-Cubs doubleheader had drifted off. The few left in the bar and poolroom, and in most of the other beer joints in southwestern Pennsylvania, were still talking baseball, but not so much about the fourth-place Pirates and their split that afternoon. They couldn't get over what had happened five days earlier, when the Boston Braves came to Pittsburgh and Babe Ruth hit three home runs, one of them over the wall, across the street and all the way into Shenley Park. It was the first time a ball had completely cleared Forbes Field.

John Plott and Ray Kunselman had stopped at the bar for a beer that warm and clear evening. Ray's girlfriend, Dorothy Horne, had come with them but decided to wait for them in the car—the 1928 Hupmobile owned by Ray's father, Elmer.

It was May 30, 1935—Memorial Day—not a particularly eventful day in Washington, Pennsylvania, but a significant one elsewhere. At 9:42 p.m., an earthquake registering 7.5 on the Richter scale killed an estimated sixty thousand people near Quetta, Pakistan. Although the Midwest was in the grip of the worst drought in its history—known as the Dust Bowl—a torrential downpour would cause the Republican River to flood, killing one hundred in eastern Colorado and southwestern Nebraska. And across the state in Philadelphia's Baker Bowl, Babe Ruth would ground out in his only appearance at the plate in what would prove to be the final game of his storied career.

Sitting at the end of the bar in Lombardo's beer joint was a man who had been drinking throughout the day. He slid over next to Plott and asked, "Have you been going around with a little fellow and his little girl in a Hupmobile car?"

Plott could tell that Ray had heard the question.

"Yes, I have been loafing around with them," Plott answered. "Well, why?"

"I want to tell you something," the man said.

"All right, what is it?"

The man took a swallow of his beer and said, "That girl gave me the clap once."

After a moment of chilly silence, Ray pushed away from the bar and faced the man.

"You're a liar," Ray said.

"I can't help it, buddy," the man said. "I can't help it if she's your sister, or your mother or your wife. She gave it to me."

"You're a liar!" Ray growled before slamming his right fist into the man's face. The man staggered backward, knocking over a stool and a chair before collapsing against the wall, unconscious.

When they reached the car, parked down at the corner of Chestnut and Jefferson Avenue, Dorothy was standing by the curb, leaning against the passenger door, smoking a cigarette.

"I just seen one of your boyfriends up there," Ray said to her. She sneered and gave him some smart remark that Plott couldn't hear, and then he slapped her hard—hard enough to knock her to the gutter.

On the day he showed up at the house on Wayne Street and threatened to shoot Iva Horne and her children, Ray Kunselman took Dorothy to Swingle's West End Hotel on Baird Avenue, where he had rented a room for her. Though she returned to her mother's home almost every day to help with the children and housework, Dorothy spent her nights at the hotel, often with Ray.

On the morning of June 5, Dorothy's friend Katherine Wilkinson stopped by the hotel to see her. It was a dingy room with a single, dusty window; the only furniture was a double bed and two cheap, battered dressers.

Ray sat, bare-chested, on the bed, smoking, while Dorothy, wearing a slip, ironed her dress. Katherine noticed that Dorothy's legs had several black and blue marks and that her lower lip was swollen. She had the feeling she had walked in on another one of their spats.

A year earlier, when Ray had made a fool of himself by falling head over heels for a girl young enough to be his child, Katherine, who had known Ray for half her life, and her husband and their friends were amused. So cute, this romance.

But as she watched them that day in their sordid little room at the West End Hotel, it was most likely evident that all the love was gone. Here was an aging man anxious to hold on to his youth and a teenager desperate to escape the drudgery of boredom and poverty. And it wasn't working.

On Wednesday, June 12, Katherine called on Dorothy at the West End Hotel at 1:30 p.m. Ray arrived a few minutes later, and Dorothy asked him for money to buy sandwiches. Ray angrily told her he had no money and left. The two women then walked to Schneider and Morrison's beer garden at the corner of McCarrell and Chestnut, where they stayed until about 4:00 p.m. before returning to Katherine's apartment to fix supper.

At about 5:00 p.m., Ray Kunselman came to the Wilkinsons' door and told Dorothy he was going to borrow some money and would return.

Ray parked in Catfish Alley and went to the rear of Tucker's beer garden, where he spoke to the owner, John Tucker, who had known Ray all his life. Ray asked to borrow twenty dollars so that he and Dorothy could take a trip to Toledo, Ohio, that night.

Tucker told Ray that he was making improvements to his building and didn't have the money to spare.

As he was leaving, Ray noticed a friend of his, Fay Aiken, entering Tucker's and followed him in. The two drank a couple of beers together, and Ray asked to borrow some money, but Aiken told him he didn't have any.

Ray drove back to the apartment, and the Wilkinsons, their young daughter and Dorothy came down to the Hupmobile to go for a ride. They drove out Route 18 south to Prosperity, turned around and came back to the apartment. At about 8:30 p.m., they all got back in the car and drove out to Taylorstown. When they returned, Katherine went upstairs to fix her husband's lunch and put her child to bed, and then the four of them drove Ray Wilkinson to his job at the Washington Tin Plate mill.

Ray, Dorothy and Katherine left the mill and drove to Schneider and Morrison's beer garden, arriving at about 11:30 p.m. Ray had no money, but he noticed that Walter Jacobs, a Lithuanian immigrant who ran a beer distributorship out of his Broad Street house, was there, and he told Katherine to ask him to come over to their booth, and maybe Jacobs would buy them some beer. Ray had seen him before, carrying a thick roll of bills.

"Do you think he has any money?" Ray asked Katherine. She said she didn't know.

The group drank heavily for the next hour. At one time, Ray and Jacobs stepped outside, and Ray asked him, "What are the chances of getting a case of beer?"

"Yes, if you have a case of empties," Jacobs answered. "You have to come to my house after it."

"I'll be over later," Ray said.

Dorothy, Katherine and Ray left the beer garden at 1:00 a.m. They stopped in front of Katherine's West Chestnut Street apartment, and Ray asked her if she wanted to go for a ride with them. Katherine said no, she had to go to bed.

Dorothy started to get out of the car, but Ray grabbed her arm and said she was going with him.

Months later, at the trial, Katherine would testify that Dorothy wanted to spend the night at Katherine's apartment but that Ray would not allow her.

That would not be the last time Katherine Wilkinson saw Dorothy Horne. But it would be the last time she saw Dorothy alive.

Death on a Red-Dog Road

George Doman had a long walk to his job at the Hazel-Atlas No. 2 glass plant in Washington, so he would always leave his Buffalo Township home in darkness. He would walk two miles along a farm road, now known as Mounts Road, until he reached Route 40—the National Pike. If he was lucky, he might hitch a ride into town, but passing cars and trucks were few and far between at that hour of the day.

On June 13, 1935, at about 4:45 a.m., as the early dawn gave a faint violet hue to the red-dog road, Doman noticed a woman's shoe lying on the right side of the road. He picked it up and kept walking. About one hundred feet farther up the road, he found another shoe, and as he bent to pick it up, he noticed that just ahead of him elderberry bushes had been bent away from the berm. He went to the spot, placed the shoes neatly on the side of the road and peered along the fence line.

The fence was old, its posts bent and wires rusted and sagging. And sprawled on those wires was the body of a girl, white and nearly naked. She lay on her back, knees slightly drawn up, her head twisted toward the ground. One of her arms stretched out; the other was at an acute angle. Her stockings were down around her ankles and her dress pulled up to her breasts. The arm of her suede jacked was ripped, and a piece of the fabric was visible several feet away.

"Halloo!" Doman said. He took hold of her knee and shook her. The flesh was cold. He shook again and got not response.

Doman then hurried up the road. When he reached Route 40 and the Ullom chicken farm (on land later occupied by the Club 40 restaurant), he turned west and headed for James McLoney's brick farmhouse because he knew the family had a telephone.

County detective Frank Creps had already put in a long day, and it was not yet 9:00 a.m. He had beaten on the door of Katherine Wilkinson's apartment until she awoke and then brought her down to the A. Blaine Day Mortuary, 52 West Maiden Street, to she if she could identify the body that had been found out in Buffalo Township.

The corpse lay on a steel, porcelain-topped table, covered by a white sheet, which Creps lifted to reveal a battered face: red bruises around the right eye and cheek, a badly swollen lip and a pea-sized bullet hole where the left temple meets the forehead, about an inch above the eye.

Katherine recoiled at the sight. She told Creps that the body was that of her friend Dorothy Horne. "But I can't hardly recognize her," she said.

The West Enders

Mounts Road in Buffalo Township, where Dorothy Horne's body was found on June 13, 1935. *Photo by the author.*

Shortly after Dorothy's mother, Iva Horne, also identified the body, George W. Ramsey, the doctor in charge of Washington Hospital's laboratory, arrived at the funeral home to perform an autopsy. He determined that the cause of death was the bullet that had traveled diagonally from the temple through the lower part of the brain, from where he removed it just below and behind the right ear.

Dr. Ramsey determined that the abrasions on her legs and the bruising and swelling on Dorothy's face had occurred shortly before her death. He testified at trial months later that a vaginal examination ordered by the district attorney's office revealed no signs of gonorrhea or sexual assault.

While the autopsy was being conducted, Creps examined the clothing removed from Dorothy's body and noticed a hole burned in the area of the left knee of her cream-colored chiffon dress. He ordered a funeral home employee to box up the clothing and keep it in a safe place.

It was pretty clear to Creps from what Iva Horne and Katherine Wilkinson had told him that the person most likely to have killed Dorothy Horne was Ray Kunselman.

Kunselman—that name again! Creps had been awakened in the wee hours of the morning by a call from the city cops. This same character had tried to rob a beer distributor—Walter Jacobs—at about 1:00 a.m. Kunselman had gotten nothing more than a dollar or two and had shot Jacobs. Miraculously, Jacobs was barely injured, the bullet having ricocheted off his belt buckle. So Kunselman was a wanted man for two separate crimes.

Even before the autopsy had been completed, Creps received a call that a car believed to be owned by Kunselman's father, Elmer, had been found about three miles from where Dorothy's body was discovered. The car had been parked between two oil wells off what is now known as Route 221, or S Bridge Road, about a quarter mile south of the intersection with the National Pike and the stone bridge built in the early 1800s in the shape of an *S* to cross a tributary of Buffalo Creek.

Creps saw in the backseat a cap and a brown overcoat, and in its pockets, he found two .32-caliber shells and a box of matches. On the floor of the front seat he found another shell, and as he bent to pick it up, he noticed what appeared to be a bullet hole in the dash. Looking at the exterior of the passenger side of the car, he discovered another hole, presumably where a bullet, fired through the dash, had exited.

When he was called to testify months later, Creps said, "There was a little blood on the floor, on the right hand side of the floor, and blood smeared on the window sill of the right front door."

That the Horne girl had been killed inside Kunselman's car was now a distinct probability. But where had Kunselman gone? The possibilities must have flashed through Creps's mind. Had he wandered off into the woods with the gun to commit suicide? Had he fled? If so, why had he abandoned his easiest means of escape? If Dr. Ramsey was correct that the girl had been killed between 1:00 and 4:00 a.m., Kunselman would have had several hours to distance himself from Washington.

Did the killer have help? Might someone have picked him up and taken him somewhere? And why would he kill her, anyway?

When he learned the Hupmobile was nearly out of gasoline, Creps had the feeling Kunselman would not get very far. Probably the only money he had was the small change he took from Jacobs, and he had even left his coat behind. It would not take long, especially with the help of the state police, to track him down, dead or alive.

Little did they know how resourceful the desperate—and very much alive—Ray Kunselman could be.

"I Must Have Been Crazy!"

Sobered by the adrenaline coursing through his body, Ray Kunselman abandoned his father's Hupmobile and walked in the direction of the National Pike, his heart pounding, his temples throbbing.

He sat beside the S Bridge, its crumbling stone walls glowing silver in the light of a waxing moon, waiting and listening for a car to come along. But it was the middle of the night, and the few vehicles that passed sped by Ray's outstretched thumb. Eventually, he began to walk north along the creek until he reached the Baltimore & Ohio tracks and then followed them toward Washington.

At daybreak, he reached a field above the Lincoln Hill coal dump and settled into the cover of bushes to sleep. He remained there until late in the evening, when he started walking into the city, toward the Hazel-Atlas No. 2 plant on South Main Street. At about 1:30 a.m. on June 14, he hopped aboard a westbound freight train that carried him to Wheeling.

In a statement he gave to District Attorney Warren Burchinal just after his arrest, Kunselman said:

> *I stayed around Wheeling for a couple of days; then I got a freight back to Washington. I stayed around the West End schoolhouse at nights. I would go around the fields and try to get something to eat at different places. I stayed there around three weeks; then I went out to Ohio. I was at Toledo, Dayton, Cincinnati and Columbus. Then I went up at Detroit...*

With school out for the summer, the Eighth Ward School (now home to an auto supply business) was a perfect hiding place. There were toilets and

The rear of the Eighth Ward School, where Ray Kunselman hid in the summer of 1935. *Photo by the author.*

running water, and it was close to the bars and restaurants frequented by Kunselman's friends and just a couple blocks from his father's house. The danger of being captured was great, but help from friends and family would keep him from starving and the other perils of life on the road.

On the afternoon of July 3, 1935, Ernest Sickles was standing outside Polan's Grocery Store at the corner of Grove Avenue and West Chestnut

Street, where he had worked for the past six years. Elmer Kunselman—Ray's father—approached him and handed him a folded piece of paper.

"Here is a note from Ray," the elder Kunselman said. "He wants to see you. He's hungry, and he wants something to eat."

Sickle and everyone else in Washington knew the younger Kunselman was the object of an intense manhunt and that aiding the suspect would be dangerous.

When Sickles got off work at 10:00 p.m. that night, he stopped for a beer at Patsy Falvo's place at the corner of Chestnut and Brookside, then headed for Tucker's beer garden, just across the street from the Eighth Ward School. Despite the risk, he bought sandwiches and ten bottles of beer and borrowed a basket in which to carry them.

Months later, at the trial, Sickles testified:

> *I walked down Catfish Alley and I went around* [back of the school] *and it was dark, and right where the doorway is there was—if there was a moon out it would be shining and light, and the instructions on the note was to go to that door, and I went to the door and I heard the latch move on it, and he opened it up and said, "Stick them up." I said, "Come on Ray, quit kidding." He said, "Oh, I was kidding, Ern."*

Sickles went into the basement, and Ray threw his arms around him and said, "Gee, I'm glad to see you, Ern. I am going crazy." Ray began to cry.

"Come on, Ray. Pull yourself together. You are a better man than that."

Ray wiped his face with his sleeve, and Sickles asked, "Why did you do that, Ray?"

"I don't know, Ern. I must have been crazy!"

"Well, tell me what happened," Sickles said.

Ray told his friend about his attempt to rob Walter Jacobs. How he went to the man's house on Broad Street and demanded the roll he had seen him carrying around. How he hit him with the gun when Jacobs claimed to have no money, and how, after Jacobs staggered toward him, he shot from the hip at him. Ray said he thought he might have killed him and ran down the street to where Dorothy was waiting in the car.

He told her what he had done, and they argued.

Ray told him that Dorothy wanted to go away with him, but he didn't want her to, and they argued about that as they drove out the pike and onto a red-dog road. They fought, and Ray took the gun and fired it once to scare her. Her dress caught fire. Then she grabbed the butt of the gun with one hand and was trying to unlatch the door with the other when, in the struggle, the gun went off and he heard her moan, heard her say, "Oh."

"She fell against the door and she fell out and he knew or thought that she was dead," Sickles would testify. "And he picked her up and then he knowed that she was dead then; he said he didn't know what to do; he said the first thought that came to his mind was to lay her over off the road."

Ray asked Sickles to bring him sandwiches, magazines, cigarettes, .32 cartridges, flashlight batteries and more beer the next day. Sickles, who had a steady job, a wife and a son, thought better of becoming more involved and did not show up. But other friends did. West Enders Val Tucker, John Plott, John Hopkins and Weldon Ewart all helped supply him with food and drink, and on July 4, some of them gave him money—enough to leave town.

Many others might not have helped the fugitive, but they were of no help to the police, either. William W. Reese was just eleven years old in 1935. "My aunts lived on Fayette Street, and I remember hearing that people would see him going into stores to buy things, see him around on the street, knew that he was sleeping in the church and the school and they kept quiet, wouldn't say anything."

Ray slipped out of Washington again after the holiday, riding the rails to Toledo, Ohio. It was there that he threw the .32-caliber revolver that had killed his lover into the muddy Maumee River. For the next three months, Ray Kunselman joined tens of thousands of other homeless men who traveled the nation in search of work. They called them hobos and tramps, these victims of the country's worst economic disaster. They had once been workers, family men—partakers of the American dream—and now many were forced to beg.

In the autumn chill of mid-October, Ray landed in Washington again. With school in session, he had no place warm to bed down. In desperation, he reached out to another friend for some special help.

Shortly after seven o'clock on the evening of October 18, Gaylord Stanley was walking into Tucker's beer garden when he heard his nickname called from the darkness by the Eighth Ward School.

"Slim!"

Stanley recognized the voice of the neighbor he had known all his life. He walked in the direction of the voice, down Catfish Alley, until a figure came into view. Ray Kunselman was wearing an old hat and a brown raincoat, and he appeared to have several other coats on beneath that.

The two talked for a while, and then Ray asked Stanley to go check the cigarette machine in Tucker's to see if the man who filled it had come yet.

Stanley did so and returned to tell the fugitive that the man must have already been there because the machine was full.

"I don't have a gun and I need one," Ray said.

"I don't have a gun," Stanley said.

"Your father has one, though."

"I can't get that because he'll miss it."

Ray reached into his pocket and took out a handmade billy club made from a large gas hose with something heavy on the end of it. He slapped it menacingly against his palm and told Stanley, "Get the gun, and I'll give it back to you."

Stanley was too scared of Ray not to obey him. The next night, Saturday, he took the .32-caliber revolver from his father's home and gave it to Ray in Catfish Alley.

Ray promised to return the gun the following night, but when Stanley went to meet him at the assigned place and time on Sunday, Ray wasn't there.

The next night, October 21, Ray was captured in Catfish Alley, carrying the loaded weapon given to him by his friend. He never used it for whatever

The courtroom where Ray Kunselman was tried for the murder of Dorothy Horne. *Photo by the author.*

purpose it was intended. It is possible that he had not committed any crime since the early morning of June 13. But the fact that he was captured with a loaded weapon made Ray Kunselman a most dangerous criminal in the eyes of the police and the public.

Ray's arrest would be front-page news, not just locally but also in Pittsburgh and beyond.

He had told his friends that what happened to Dorothy Horne was an accident, but the authorities had a different opinion.

Ray Kunselman was charged with first-degree murder, and if convicted, his death in the electric chair would be almost certain.

On Trial for Murder

In our own time, the wheels of justice grind exceedingly slowly. Trials might follow indictments many months and even years later. Many convicts sentenced to death never exhaust their appeals before dying of other causes. But in 1935, those wheels flew along greased rails. Ray Kunselman found himself on trial for murder in the Washington County Courthouse, before the massive mahogany desk of Judge Howard W. Hughes, exactly four weeks after his arrest on a dark and rain-soaked alley in Washington's West End.

Jury selection began on Monday morning, November 18, a frigid day on which the temperature would reach only twenty-seven degrees. By lunchtime Tuesday, twelve jurors had been chosen from a pool of seventy-one. Thirteen of the prospective jurors were dismissed because they expressed disapproval of the death penalty.

Four of the five female jurors were described as housekeepers; the fifth was a widow. Two male jurors were farmers, and the others included a clerk, a glassworker, a laborer, an engineer and a tobacco salesman.

Earle Forrest, a veteran reporter, covered the trial for both the *Observer* and the *Reporter*. When Iva Rafferty Horne, the mother of the victim, took the stand, Forrest wrote:

> *A frail little woman of thirty-five years, with a pale, careworn face, she has seen much suffering which has aged her beyond her years. Dressed in plain dark brown, she presented a pathetic picture as she sat there and in a voice scarcely audible told a story of how she had tried to keep her daughter at*

These photographs of the principals in Kunselman's trial were first published in the *Pittsburgh Press* and later in the local Washington newspapers. *Courtesy of Observer Publishing Co.*

home and had finally ordered Ray Kunselman to keep away after he was beating her in the kitchen of their home in Wayne Street.

The *Pittsburgh Press* described Mrs. Horne as "poorly dressed in somber clothes, with cheeks sunken," and she "chewed gum slyly."

District Attorney Warren S. Burchinal had been confident of victory for the prosecution going into the trial, but his case for first-degree murder was not so strong. Kunselman, in giving his statement, had lied about the gun he was carrying when he was arrested. Going into the trial, Burchinal assumed he had the murder weapon, but he did not; that gun, as he later learned, was resting on the bottom of the Maumee River in Toledo, Ohio.

Burchinal also could not establish a motive. Throughout the trial, he portrayed the defendant as a ruthless brute, a jealous woman-beater who lacked conscience and compassion. But the testimony of the West Enders called to the stand painted Kunselman as someone not much different from them or his victim: impulsive, irresponsible and drunk half the time. He would need to convince the jury that Ray was not typical and that he had destroyed Dorothy Virginia Horne's innocence before degrading and, eventually, killing her.

Ray's attorney, Thomas L. Christman, was confident that the jury would decide his client's action amounted to nothing more serious than manslaughter. He pecked away at the credibility of the prosecution witnesses, mostly Ray's friends, who had all broken the law by assisting the fugitive but would escape charges because of their testimony. Furthermore, there was no evidence presented of premeditation.

On Thursday, November 1, the courthouse, cavernous beneath an ornate ceiling, was packed with spectators, as it had been all week. Mary Turner, Ray's sister, and his father sat directly behind the defense table. "And in another chair just back of the district attorney," wrote Forrest, "was the figure of a little woman, pale and careworn whose eyes seldom left Kunselman's face as he told his story. This was Mrs. Iva Horne, mother of the dead girl."

In front of this audience, Ray maintained his tough-guy demeanor. As he took the stand, "he swaggered as he walked," wrote Forrest. "This air of bravado that he evidently did not feel was apparent all through his direct examination, for he was having his 'day in court.'"

Under questioning from his attorney, Kunselman gave his version of the events of June 12 and of the robbery of Walter Jacobs and his flight from town with Dorothy. He testified that he had tried to get her to leave the car, but she refused. They drove several miles west before Kunselman turned left on what is now Mounts Road, and they continued to argue and hit each other until he stopped the car about a mile from the main highway. Their fighting continued, and then Kunselman picked up the gun that was on the seat between them and fired it into the dashboard. The flash caused Dorothy's dress to smoke, and he slapped out the fire with his palm.

"Well, I told her I was going to go," Kunselman testified. "I told her I didn't know what I was going to do with her. She wanted to go, and she even cried to go along. I told her that I couldn't take her. I didn't have no money or gasoline. Then we got to chewing the rag there, and she reached over and I smacked her, and she was wrestling the gun around and so was I, and she grabbed hold of the gun and I grabbed her hand."

Christman said, "Go ahead, Ray. Tell us what happened from then on."

> *Well, she was moving around, wrestling there, and all I can remember, it seemed like she was trying to open the door with her right hand and I had hold of her hand like that and she had hold of the gun, the butt end, and while we were wrestling there and jerking around, she seemed to lean over a little like that, just as the gun went off, and I heard her go "Oh" and the door came open at the same time and she fell out in the road. Well, I wasn't drunk, what you would say clear drunk, but I had enough to make me crazy and simple or whatever it was...I got out; she fell down beside the car. I got out and jumped down off the running board and I straddled her with my legs and reached in under her, under her breasts and I don't know about anybody being dead. I thought she was dead and I got my hands under her breast and mover her over onto the bank, if there was a bank there; it was too dark to tell.*

The jurors had heard this same version of events from several of the witnesses; they would get a different version during the withering cross-examination.

Burchinal introduced as evidence two photos of Dorothy found in the defendant's wallet, with "I love you" written on one of them. The following Q&A is from the trial transcript:

> Q: And you loved her?
> A: Yes.
> Q: Loved her dearly?
> A: I guess I did...too much.
> Q: Crazy about her?
> A: Yes, I was.
> Q: Jealous about her?

District attorney Warren Burchinal. *Courtesy of Observer Publishing Co.*

A: No, not exactly that.

Q: But you loved her enough that on every provocation you smacked her, didn't you?

A: No, I didn't.

Q: The night or the early morning of the 13th, when you were out along the road with her parked in the car, you were in love with her then, weren't you?

A: Yes, sir.

Q: But you smacked her time after time, didn't you?

A: Yes, I did.

Q: That was your way of showing her how much you were in love with her, was it?

A: She never objected.

Burchinal hammered away at the defendant without mercy. His strategy was to create a much different scenario, one in which Kunselman took the victim against her will onto a road he was quite familiar with, where he beat her and punished her, intending all along to kill her and then did so deliberately.

In closing arguments, wrote Forrest, "Christman made a gallant fight for the life of the defendant…and made a strong plea that under the evidence the defendant was guilty of manslaughter only."

The jury heard Christman conclude, "You don't have to answer to me. You don't have to answer to Mr. Burchinal. You have to answer only to God."

Burchinal, in his closing statement, said, "The body of that poor, defenseless nineteen-year-old girl is the worst witness against that man who sits there, trying to save his own life by a lie."

Judge Hughes, in his charge to the jury, gave broad definitions of "malice" and "intent," and in doing so, he seemed to support the commonwealth's case:

> *Where a person uses a deadly weapon without a sufficient cause of provocation, he must be presumed to do it wickedly or from a bad heart, so, he who takes the life of another with a deadly weapon and with a manifest design to use it upon him or upon her, as it was in this case, with sufficient time to deliberate and fully to form the conscious purpose of killing, and without any sufficient reason or cause of extenuation, is guilty of murder in the first degree.*

But the judge gave the jury much more to think about, saying that if the jurors believed Dorothy's finger was on the trigger and that her actions led to her own death, then they must find the defendant not guilty.

The West Enders

In conclusion, Hughes instructed the jury that if it should decide on murder in the first degree, it must choose between the death sentence and life in prison.

The jury began its deliberations at 12:10 p.m. on Friday, November 22. Rumors spread along courthouse hallways that the jury was split in some way. By 7:00 p.m., the impasse still had not been broken; dinner was ordered. At some point during the meal, an agreement was reached, and at 8:10 p.m., the jurors sent word that they were ready to return.

The courtroom was nearly empty of spectators, Mary Turner, Kunselman's sister, being one of the few remaining.

"Members of the jury, have you agreed upon a verdict?" the clerk asked.

"We have," the jurors responded.

"Who shall speak for you?" the clerk asked.

The foreman, tobacco salesman J.L. Page, indicated he would.

"Look upon the defendant, you that are sworn, and say that he is guilty or not guilty of the felony whereof he stands indicted."

Page looked into the eyes of Ray Kunselman, standing at the defense table. "We find the defendant guilty of murder in the first degree," he said.

"Kunselman seemed to waiver slightly," Forrest wrote later.

"And we fix the penalty at life imprisonment," Page added after a short pause.

The defendant closed his eyes and appeared to be relieved.

It would later be revealed that jurors had decided on a first-degree murder conviction early in the deliberation but had split, six to six, on whether Kunselman should die for his crime. Over dinner, mercy won out.

Only two people knew for sure what happened on that lonely stretch of red-dog road in Buffalo Township in the early morning hours of June 13, 1935. One of them was dead, and the other would be confined to a cell with that secret for the rest of his life.

Sheriff's deputies grasped Kunselman by the arms just above his elbows and led him from the courtroom, his knees buckling slightly, his lower lip trembling, all his West End swagger gone.

Three days later, on Monday, November 23, the murder of Dorothy Horne was no longer front-page news. Another violent crime had not just grabbed the headlines but also merited an extra edition of the *Reporter*. While her fourteen-year-old son, home from school ill, slept upstairs in their Springfield Avenue home, Pearl Dille, twenty-nine, was shot to death downstairs by Lloyd Andrews, thirty-eight, who then turned the gun on himself. Other news, too, grabbed readers' attention: Italy's invasion of Ethiopia and Washington & Jefferson College's humiliating 55–0 loss to West Virginia University and Wash High's 39–6 victory over rival Canonsburg in Saturday football games.

As Kunselman awaited sentencing, Japan continued to penetrate China; Marie, the littlest of the Dionne quintuplets, took her first steps; and President Roosevelt, in a forceful reply to New Deal critics, told a crowd of ninety thousand that lavish government spending was over and that the nation could "look forward with assurance to a decreasing deficit."

On December 7, the day Kunselman left the county jail for his new home at Western State Penitentiary, the Marx Brothers' movie *A Night at the Opera* opened at the State Theater in Washington.

Life went on in the West End, pretty much as it always had, as its inhabitants found other topics to talk about. The passion, the fury and the desperation that led to the tragedy of Ray Kunselman and Dorothy Horne would settle in corners of the memories of those who had known them, later to be lost to time.

Epilogue

The beer gardens, the Swingle Hotel and almost all of the other places into which Ray and Dorothy stepped are gone now. Still, the character of the West End is not so different. Gone, too, are the memories of the people most involved in their drama.

James Armour, the patrolman who captured the fugitive in Catfish Alley, would later be promoted to sergeant. He retired from the force after World War II and then worked as a watchman for Harper Feed Mills.

Thomas Chistman, Kunselman's attorney, would go on to defend Robert Dreamer, accused of killing teenager Thelma Young, in another high-profile murder trial held the following spring.

Warren Burchinal left the district attorney's office and returned to private practice. He died in 1967 at the age of seventy-seven. In his lifetime, he was not nearly as well known as his son, General David Burchinal, who went on to command U.S. forces in Europe.

Judge Howard Wingett Hughes, like Burchinal a Washington & Jefferson College graduate, was appointed in 1943 to fill a vacancy on the Pennsylvania Supreme Court. On June 20, 1945, while serving as general solicitor for the Pennsylvania Railroad, he stepped out of his residence in Philadelphia's Warwick Hotel and dropped dead on the sidewalk. He was fifty-three.

After his wife, Etta, died giving birth to their sixth child, Elmer Kunselman had to raise Ray and his other children on his own, according to his cousin, Grace Livingood, who was eleven years old at the time of the trial and has lived in the same house on Fayette Street since she was born. "He was so hurt. He tried so hard to talk to Ray, but Ray just wanted to drink," she said.

"Uncle Elmer was such a good man," Mrs. Livingood said. "He never said anything bad about anybody, and he never talked about it with anyone. He took it so hard. He was never the same after that."

Iva Horne was later married to Mead McMillen and moved to the Erie area, where she lived to be ninety-eight and died in 1996.

Dorothy Horne was buried in Immaculate Conception Cemetery.

Dorothy Horne's grave in Immaculate Conception Cemetery. *Photo by the author.*

Ray Kunselman's grave in Washington Cemetery. *Photo by the author.*

Ray Kunselman was taken to Western State Penitentiary on December 8, 1935. According to Joseph Horne, Kunselman wrote to his mother about ten years later, asking her forgiveness and seeking her help in arranging his parole. She refused. In January 1954, he was transferred to Rockview State Penitentiary in Bellefonte, where he died in 1955.

Ray Kunselman is buried in Washington Cemetery in the family plot beside his sister Mary and his father—the two people who never gave up believing that what had occurred that early morning of June 13, 1935, was not murder but rather a tragic collision of souls.

5
THE WRECK OF THE CANNONBALL EXPRESS

In the 1820s, the nation's traffic westward came straight through Washington County along the newly constructed National Pike, which started in Cumberland, Maryland, and eventually terminated in Vandalia, Illinois. Thirty years later, the number of wagons passing through its toll booths and over its S bridges would drop dramatically as a faster, more efficient form of transportation came into being: railroads.

Before long, it would be possible to travel by rail between towns of any notable size in Washington County. The technological and social changes were startling; a journey that would have taken more than a week just a few years earlier could now be undertaken in a matter of hours.

By 1888, the Baltimore & Ohio tracks came down from Pittsburgh into Finleyville; then headed westward to Washington; on to Wheeling, West Virginia, and Cincinnati, Ohio; and eventually reached St. Louis, Missouri. The Chartiers Valley Railroad came down from Pittsburgh to Washington through Canonsburg. The Steubenville and Pittsburgh line ran through Burgettstown and McDonald in northern Washington County, and the narrow-gauge Washington & Waynesburg Railroad serviced those two boroughs and all the villages in between.

The railroads, along with the discovery of huge deposits of coal, oil and gas in Washington County, would open a sleepy, agricultural region to the world and transform its county seat into an industrial boomtown. Progress came with great speed, and safety trailed far behind. Fatal accidents became common in both the new industries and on the tracks.

S.G. Rogers made this photograph of the wreckage of the Cannonball Express on October 19, 1888. *Courtesy of Observer Publishing Co.*

Although the Baltimore & Ohio Railroad's Cannonball Express was so named for its speed, the train running from Cincinnati, Ohio, to Pittsburgh, Pennsylvania, was well behind schedule when it pulled into the station at Columbus on October 19, 1888. George W. Matthews, conductor of the Pullman sleeper, stepped down to the platform at 2:30 a.m. that Friday morning in order to greet the three passengers he had been told to expect, one of whom was so widely known as to make the conductor anxious. Presently, two gentlemen in topcoats stepped out of the depot, and Matthews ordered his porter, Amos Ford, to take their luggage to the baggage car.

Matthews helped the men aboard and showed them to their berths in the crowded sleeper. The younger of the two, James W. Batchelor, sixty, took an upper berth on the station side. His brother, Captain Charles W. Batchelor, sixty-five, readied himself to climb into the opposite lower berth, but Matthews, much embarrassed in the presence of these distinguished passengers, apologized and informed him it had been reserved for another, a woman who had yet to board. It became apparent, however, as the train prepared to depart the station that she would not arrive, and Matthews, much to his relief, secured the captain in the lower berth and then climbed

The Wreck of the Cannonball Express

into the bunk above him—the last unoccupied one of the twenty-two in the car—for a few blessed hours of rest. He would awaken less than five hours later to find his world quite literally turned upside down.

Captain Batchelor had not been at the helm of a riverboat for more than thirty years, but he would proudly retain the title for the rest of his life. His youthful experiences on the Ohio and Mississippi Rivers were no less romantic and adventurous than those of his contemporary Mark Twain, and the title kept him forever connected to it. Though he had reached the highest degree as a Mason and accumulated a fortune later in life as a businessman, industrialist and bank president, he never lost his love and longing for the river.

Captain Batchelor and his brother had actually begun their journey from Cincinnati at 11:00 a.m. the previous day, accompanied by the captain's wife, Mary, and their grandnephew, Jamie, but the brothers had stepped off the train in Columbus in order to conduct some business regarding their investments in the Ohio oilfields and allowed their relations to continue home ahead of them.

The captain's trip was tinged with irony. He had been part owner of a steamer called the *Allegheny* and had steered it along the Ohio River from Pittsburgh to Cincinnati many times. But in 1852, when the B&O opened its route between the cities, Batchelor feared the competition. He gave up his command of the boat in 1853 and sold his interest to his partners the following year. And now the car, rocking from its speed, was pulling him out of the past and into a future where the majestic riverboat would be obsolete.

Some of the other passengers who had been awakened by the stop in Columbus and the commotion in the sleeper that followed were just then dropping off to sleep. In the lower berth to the rear of the captain slept Stephen Collins, a man nearly as well known as Batchelor in Pittsburgh, where he served as supervisor of the mails. In the berth below James Batchelor lay Mr. and Mrs. W.S. Greer. The husband and wife were on their way from Dodge City, Kansas, where Greer was employed by the Santa Fe Railroad, to Pittsburgh to visit Mrs. Greer's mother. The journey, which had already been a long and uncomfortable one for the Greers, would be over in just a few short hours.

Or so they thought.

The train was just under an hour behind schedule when engineer James Noonan pulled Locomotive Engine No. 427 into the station at Cambridge, Ohio, where half a dozen passengers waited patiently on the platform in the predawn chill. The train was not a long one. Behind the engine and

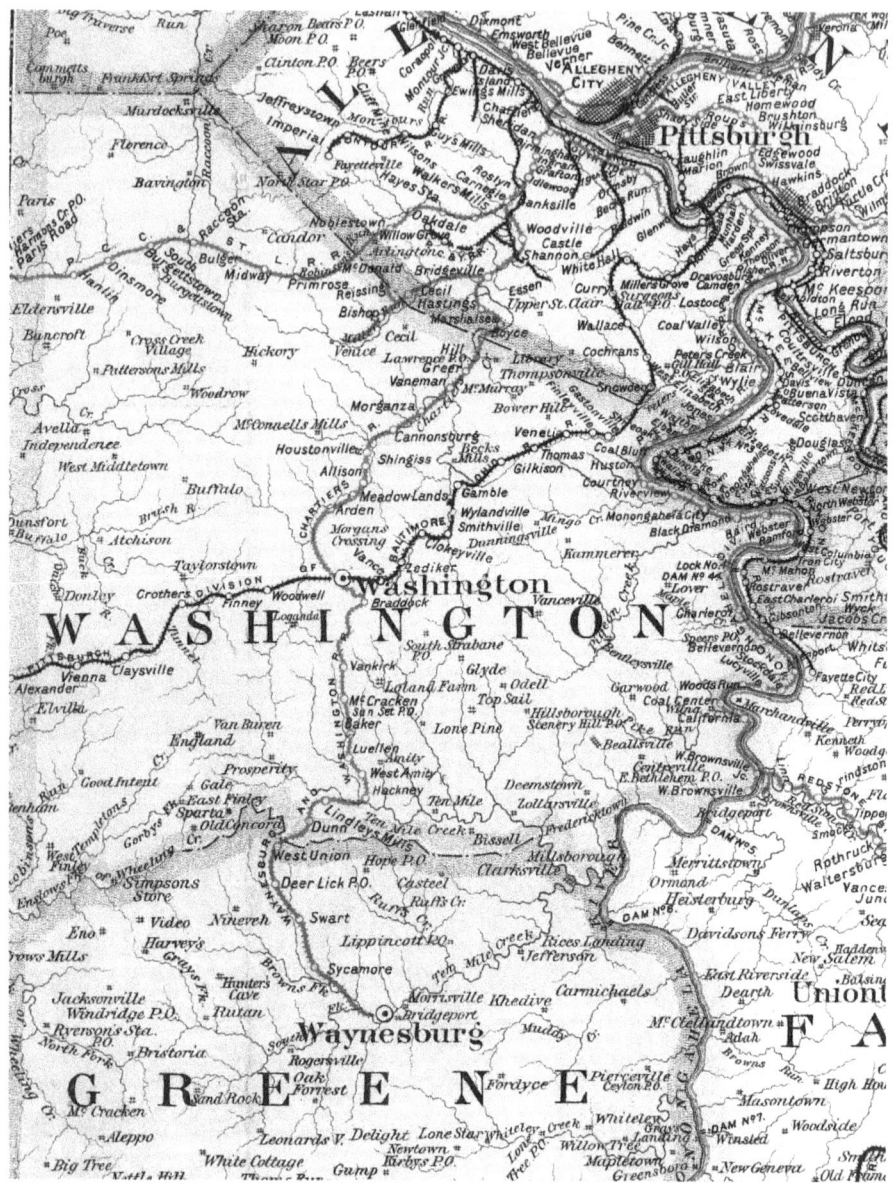

A map showing the railroads as they existed in Washington County in 1895. *Library of Congress, Geography and Map Division.*

its tender were, in order, a refrigerated car carrying fruit, the baggage car, the Pullman sleeper ("Monroeville" and "No. 714" painted in gold lettering along its side) and two passenger coaches.

The Wreck of the Cannonball Express

Conductor David Francis helped some of the travelers mount the steps to the forward coach, the "ladies' car." Among them was an elderly New Concord woman, Hannah McKinney, en route to visit her son, a minister in Beaver Falls, northwest of Pittsburgh. Also requiring some help with her bags was Nettie Pringle McConkey and her two youngest children, six-year-old Walter and one-year-old Frederick. She was the wife of the Reverend William J. McConkey, a Cambridge native and graduate of Jefferson College in Canonsburg who had become a Presbyterian minister in Grove City. His wife was from New Concord, not far from Cambridge, and was returning home after a visit with relatives. Conductor Francis found Mrs. McConkey and her children a comfortable seat next to the coal stove so that she might keep the baby warm.

The engineer, James Noonan, and his fireman, William McAuliffe, both thirty-three years old, hoped to make up some time between Cambridge and Wheeling. With a little luck, they might be at their homes in Glenwood, not far from Pittsburgh, for a late breakfast. They would never make it that far.

An Open Switch

The Cannonball began its long ascent from Wheeling and the Ohio River Valley as dawn broke, one hour and thirty-five minutes behind time. Meanwhile, in Washington, some B&O employees were taking the opportunity of the delay to move an engine off the main track and into what was called the "Y," a diversion used to turn around locomotives (see map on page 104). The Y could be accessed by a switch off the main track from either direction. The two branches of the Y converged at what is now South Franklin Street, the stem of the Y leading toward the center of town.

Conductor Cornelius Heck directed brakeman Edward Boon to open the west switch to allow his engine, tender and caboose onto the Y. Boon, who had grown up on a farm in Buffalo Township, was still in his apprenticeship, having started work for the railroad less than two months earlier. "I opened the switch to let the engine on the Y, jumped on the pilot of the engine and rode up the track," Boon would later testify. "I had forgotten that I had left the switch open. I thought that some of the other brakemen had closed it. I don't always close the switches I open. The end brakeman usually closes the switches. It is the duty of all conductors to see to all the switches; it's in the book of rules."

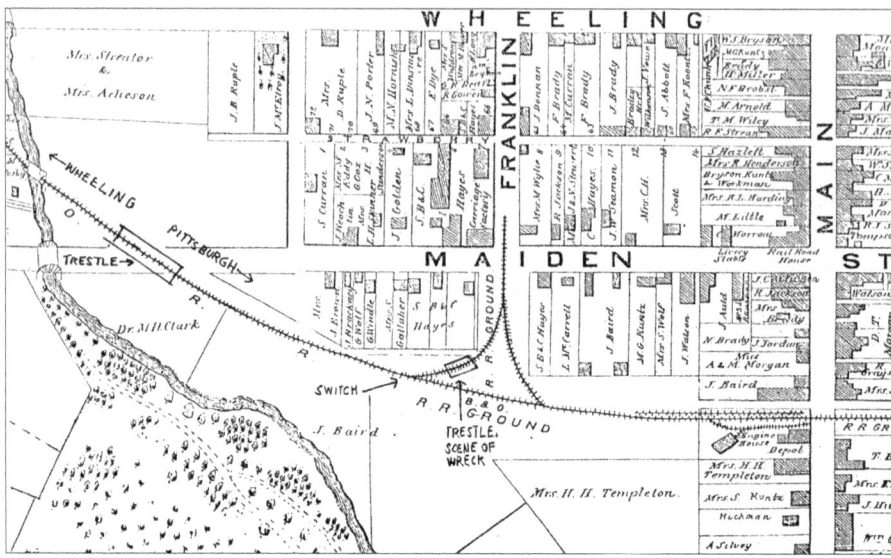

This map shows the "Y" used to turn around engines and the trestle there from which the train plunged. *From* Caldwell's Illustrated Atlas of Washington County.

Meanwhile, the Cannonball flew eastward through West Alexander, Coon Island, Taylorstown, Coffey's Crossing and, finally, Lincoln Hill, where engineer Noonan began to ease the throttle, the depot at Washington just a little more than a mile away.

The switch was equipped with a signal to alert approaching trains of its position, but as would be stated at a later inquest, the signal was poorly situated and not visible at all to the engineer in his position. "The fireman could have seen it if he had been looking for it about half way across the [first] trestle," J.H. Jamison, supervisor of trains and engines, would later testify. The fireman, McAuliffe, apparently was not looking, but Jamison said that even if he had seen it, engineer Noonan would not have been able to stop the train in time. Cannonball conductor Francis, who was riding in the last car, guessed the train was traveling at twenty miles per hour at 7:50 a.m. when it reached the first trestle, which is still used today and carries tracks over West Maiden Street.

As soon as the leading wheels turned into the switch, Noonan, realizing what had happened, reversed the engine and put on the air brakes, but nothing could stop what was about to happen. With a deafening screech the behemoth machine leaned through the tight turn of the Y and, as its left wheels lifted from the rail, began to plunge to the right just as it crossed another trestle, this one carrying the track twelve feet above ground.

The Wreck of the Cannonball Express

A Moment of Terror

Matthews, conductor of the Pullman sleeper, would later recall:

> *Just before reaching Washington I had thrown back the blankets, as it was very warm, and was about to arise. Just then I felt the car jarring and immediately after felt it falling. I thought we had gone off the big trestle below Washington and gave up all hope. But the car hit so soon I knew we had not tumbled off the big trestle. The lights went out and I felt myself flying against the seats in the overturned car.*

The refrigerated freight car followed the engine over the smaller trestle and then the baggage car, whose roof and sides were torn away as it was pulled off the rails, catapulting baggage master James Henry forty feet from the tracks. A heavy trunk was sailing right behind him and landed on him, crushing his chest—an injury from which he would recover.

Pullman passenger Collins was well acquainted with train wrecks, having survived four others. "I had been thinking of the fast time being made on such a rough road, and the swinging of the car was simply fearful all night," he would later tell a staff writer for the *Reporter*.

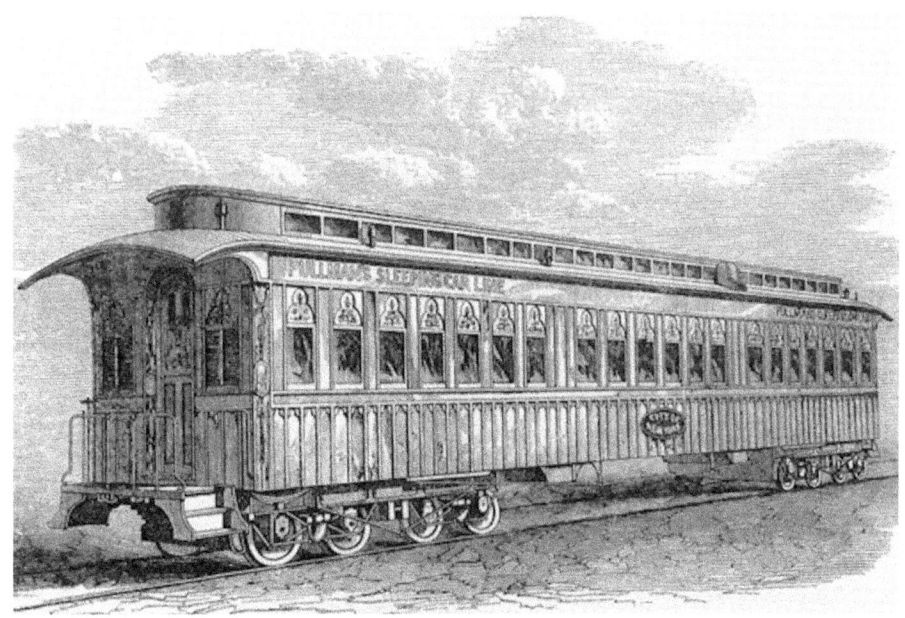

A Pullman sleeper car, circa 1876. *American Science and Invention.*

So accustomed, however, had I become to the motion that when the accident occurred and the train left the track, I merely thought it was another and greater jolt. But in a moment a terrific shock followed, in turn succeeded by a crushing, grinding noise, simply horrifying. You've never been in a railroad wreck? Well, then, you cannot imagine the awful sound, a thousand times louder than any thunder ever heard.

Matthews was knocked senseless by a blow to the head. "When I recovered I thought of the heating apparatus. I knew what the result would be if the car caught fire." Before he could reach the end of the car, windows were smashed in, and he was dragged to safety by his porter, Amos Ford, who had suffered a deep wound on his forehead. "I must say he did good work," Matthews said later. "He labored like a Trojan." As was the custom of the time, the newspaper was obliged to parenthetically describe Ford as "colored."

A gash was ripped in Collins's leg when he was thrown from his berth:

When my senses returned I was covered with blood from head to foot. My shirt, underclothes and socks were saturated with the gore while a three-inch wound in my head yawned, and its appearance, judging from the fact that a lady fainted as soon as she saw me, must have been anything but pleasing.

Mrs. McConkey's baby was asleep on her lap, and her son, Walter, was curled up on the seat beside her when the first passenger coach dove from the tracks. The stove was upset, and the burning coal spewing from it set fire to the woman's dress. Almost at the same time, however, in what would later be called a miracle, the car's water cooler was upset. It's contents fell in the direction of the fire, drowning it out and extinguishing the burning clothing. Mrs. McConkey was burned slightly on the arm and leg and her baby on the ear and knee, but young Walter escaped injury. Had the fire not been doused, it would have quickly spread through the crowded car, and the loss of life would have been great.

Other passengers in the car were not as lucky as the McConkey family. The elderly Mrs. McKinney lay twisted between the seats, unconscious, her ribs broken. The screams of Michael Stanton, with both his arms broken and his leg snapped above the knee, could be heard above the din as rescuers attempted to remove him from the car.

The wreckage was quickly surrounded by hundreds of townspeople, many of them helping to rescue passengers, others there to gawk and collect

The Wreck of the Cannonball Express

This photo by S.G. Rogers shows the last coach, in which not one of the passengers was seriously injured. *Courtesy of Observer Publishing Co.*

souvenirs. Young boys ran about with bunches of grapes that had spilled from the freight car.

The body of engineer Noonan, married and the father of three children, lay crushed beneath the steaming wreckage of the locomotive and would not be recovered until hours later. The gravely injured fireman McAuliffe was removed immediately and taken to the waiting room of the depot on South Main Street and later to a room at Bryson Brothers furniture store, where he would be pronounced dead at two thirty that afternoon.

Most of the passengers in the last coach, which had only tipped and not gone down over the trestle, were not injured and walked to the waiting room of the station, where they might catch another train for Pittsburgh. Some of the more than twenty passengers hurt also made their way in that direction, including Mr. and Mrs. Greer, the couple from Dodge City, who had both suffered bruises. Presently, however, Mrs. Greer began to experience severe pain of the spine and was taken, along with her husband, to the home of John Baird, which stood where city hall is now located. Mrs. McKinney had been admitted there, as well, as were Mr. and Mrs. A. Kaufman of New York City.

William Smith opened his five rooms above Isadore Schoenthal's store at the southeast corner of Main and Wheeling Streets as a temporary hospital, the borough not having any such facility. Other residents, too, readily opened their homes to the injured.

James Batchelor was taken unconscious from the wreckage of the Pullman car to the home of Patrick J. Finn, a grocer. Although he had suffered no visible wounds, his injuries were judged to be grave. His older brother was discovered unhurt in the station's waiting room.

A reporter for the local newspaper went to the home of Captain Batchelor in Pittsburgh that night and spoke with his daughter, Lillie B. Campau, about how her father had managed to avoid being hurt.

"Papa didn't remember anything," said Mrs. Campau, "until he found himself sitting in the waiting room at Washington. How the accident happened, or how he was extricated, he doesn't know."

A LIFE OF ADVENTURE

It is not difficult to conjure the sight of Captain Batchelor sitting in the waiting room of the Washington depot, disheveled and only partly dressed, bits of debris lodged in his long, gray beard. Nor is it difficult to imagine what might have been going through his mind then. This was not his only close call, his only near escape from death.

Captain Charles W. Batchelor. *Courtesy of University of Pittsburgh Library.*

Just a year before this accident, Captain Batchelor, a native of Steubenville, Ohio, had published his autobiography, in which he recollected his adventures on the river and in the world of business. President Lincoln appointed him as surveyor of the Port of Pittsburgh, he was president of the Pittsburgh Petroleum Exchange and he was credited with bringing natural gas for manufacturing to Pittsburgh and Wheeling. But his earlier exploits on the water probably made for more interesting reading.

In 1852, he was traveling with his wife on the steamer *Henry Clay* from Albany to New York City when their boat was damaged while racing with another down the Hudson River, just north of Yonkers. Fire spread quickly from the engine room as the skipper aimed it for the rocky western shore. Batchelor took his wife to the bow, and when the boat grounded on a sandbar, he lowered Mary as far over the side as he could before dropping her and then followed. They survived uninjured, but eight fellow passengers died by fire or drowning.

As he wrote in *Incident in the Life of Charles W. Batchelor*, when he commanded the riverboat *Americus* on the Illinois River, swollen with floodwater in 1855, one of his crew alerted him of a person hailing the ship from the shore. The *Monongahela Daily Republican*, in an obituary published on June 30, 1896, described the event:

> *The boat ran ashore in answer to the signal, when the passenger was found to be a ministerial looking man on a white horse. The pilot, who had the utmost faith in the old saying that "a parson and a white horse would sink a boat," besought Capt. Batchelor to continue down the river without the steed and his rider, warning him that unless he did disaster would be sure to overtake the boat.*
>
> *Capt. Batchelor laughed at his fears, and the minister was taken aboard. About four o'clock that afternoon the boat took fire and burned to the water's edge. It was the last steamer Capt. Batchelor ever commanded.*

Captain Batchelor was reunited with his brother later that morning at the Finn residence. James was carried by stretcher to the Chartiers station at the foot of South Main Street and put aboard the 1:50 p.m. train to Pittsburgh, where the family, doctors and, perhaps, an undertaker anxiously awaited his arrival.

Fear, Grief and Blame

James Batchelor was not the only passenger thought to be near death. Jacob Sigel, who lay in the Auld House hotel at the northwest corner of Main and Maiden Streets, was so fearful of dying that he called for a lawyer to draw up his will.

Sigel, from Allegheny City, was a passenger in the Pullman sleeper. He had risen, dressed and was getting his baggage from porter Amos Ford when the car careened from the trestle. His right ankle was crushed and dislocated, his back sprained and his head badly cut.

James Franklin Taylor, district attorney for Washington County, arrived late Thursday morning at the Auld House and drew up Sigel's will. Sigel also asked to see a trustworthy person with whom he might entrust his valuables. The Reverend J.F. Jones was summoned, to whom Sigel turned over $5,000 in cash and other valuables. That sum in today's dollar would be enormous considering that total damages to the railroad from the wreck were estimated at $25,000. By the next morning, however, when his wife arrived on the train from Pittsburgh, Sigel, a Civil War veteran, was feeling much better.

Not much was known about the dead fireman, William McAuliffe, other than the fact that he was a Mason. The Odd Fellows Lodge in Washington offered its assistance, and its treasurer, John M. Cook, was able to determine that although the single man was living in Glenwood, near Pittsburgh, his hometown was Oxford, in southern New York State, about fifteen miles west of the Hudson River. Cook and McAuliffe's roommate in Glenwood, William Wells, accompanied the body there to be received by McAuliffe's aged parents, who had relied on their son's salary for their support.

After the funeral on Monday, October 22, Cook conveyed to the couple from the railroad $10 from McAuliffe's last pay. They would also be the beneficiaries of their son's $1,000 life insurance policy.

Although the engineer, James Noonan, was also living in Glenwood for his work, his wife, the former Carrie Shively, and three children were in their hometown of Connellsville, Fayette County, and that is where the funeral took place on Sunday. More than one hundred engineers from all over the region attended, and free transportation was offered to all railroad employees who wished to go, a decision that essentially shut down freight traffic for the day.

With men working around the clock, by noon on Monday, October 22, most of the wreckage had been cleared. The most seriously injured passengers were all doing better, and all were expected to survive. James Batchelor had undergone surgery and remained in Mercy Hospital in Pittsburgh but was expected to return home later in the week. Mrs. Greer, having suffered a severe contusion of the spine, was resting at the home of her mother. Henry, the baggage master, was in great pain from broken ribs but out of danger. Conductor Matthews was stiff and sore but otherwise mobile.

The *Reporter*, so busy relating the facts, became just as busy dousing rumors. "Some most horrible stories have been told concerning a baby that was one of the passengers in the wreck," it reported in its Monday afternoon edition. "One was to the effect it had been burned to death; another that the porter had fallen over on it, crushing out its life; still another that its hair had been pulled out by the roots. There is no foundation whatever for these statements."

Because Coroner J.F. Kennedy was ill and at home in Union Township, Justice of the Peace C.M. Ruple was appointed Saturday to be acting coroner and met that day in his office with District Attorney Taylor and M.C. Acheson, attorney for the B&O Railroad. They heard the testimony of witnesses, toured the wreckage site, examined the switch and adjourned until Monday morning.

Ruple and the six men sworn as jurors concluded that the novice brakeman, Edward Boon, was criminally negligent and that conductor Cornelius Heck should be charged with involuntary manslaughter in the death of the two trainmen. They also determined fault on the part of the railroad for maintaining a trestle that was "extremely dangerous whether a train runs into it rapidly or slowly." In its verdict, the jury also found "gross negligence on the part of B&O Railroad Company in not having provided adequate signals at this point so that engineers of trains may know without mistake whether the said switch is open or closed."

Heck, who had been fired by the railroad two days after the wreck, was thought to have gone to his home in Punxatawney, Pennsylvania. In accordance with the verdict, Ruple issued a warrant for his arrest.

The Common Calamity

Fatal accidents involving trains and trolleys were not unusual in the late nineteenth century; in fact, in Washington County, the newspapers reported them almost daily. Most of the deaths involved people falling from trains or being struck while crossing tracks or walking, sitting or sleeping on them, not from derailments, which were nevertheless frequent. Though safety improvements were made to tracks and signals in the wake of the event of October 19, 1888, crashes continued to happen. In May 1896, the Cannonball Express from Cincinnati to Pittsburgh wrecked again, this time three miles east of Washington, when an axle on the locomotive broke, killing fireman Patrick Flaherty.

As common as railroad deaths were, it is not surprising that the attention of newspaper readers in Washington quickly turned away from the 1888 wreck of the Cannonball Express and the injured to topics of more interest. It was a presidential election year, after all, and political fever was high in the county that autumn. Special trains were arranged to take supporters of Republican Benjamin Harrison and Democrat Grover Cleveland to massive rallies. The *Reporter*, a Republican voice and opponent of Cleveland's free-trade policies, ignored the Democrats' rallies but publicized the Republicans'. Though Harrison would lose the popular vote, he would win a majority of electoral votes in November. He took Washington County and Pennsylvania easily.

The story that had dominated the front pages of newspapers for weeks before the wreck of the Cannonball and for weeks after it had nothing to do with either politics or railroads; rather, it was the sensational murder trial of Van Baker. Baker was a schoolteacher and native of Cross Creek in Washington County who had been living in Holiday's Cove, West Virginia, where he was superintendent of schools. After an extended visit

This piece of the brass bell from Engine No. 427 was found in files at the *Observer-Reporter* kept by historian Earle Forrest. *Photo by the author.*

The Wreck of the Cannonball Express

to Cross Creek, Baker allegedly returned home in May 1887 to find his wife, Eliza Jane, forty-five, and her mother, Drusilla McWha, seventy, butchered with an axe. The murders had occurred more than a month earlier, on April 9, 1887. In late October 1888, Baker was found guilty of first-degree murder in a Wellsburg, West Virginia courtroom and sentenced to life in prison.

Captain C.W. Batchelor would continue to have an active life until his death in June 1896. An Ohio River steamboat was named after him. His brother, James, died in October 1909 at the age of seventy-nine.

Nettie McConkey's two youngest children would follow in their father's footsteps. Walter Pringle McConkey, just six years old when the Cannonball Express crashed, graduated from Grove City College in 1903 and entered the ministry. He would become pastor of Central Presbyterian Church in Pittsburgh. The baby, Frederick Paul McConkey, graduated from Grove City in 1909. He received his doctorate in divinity from Princeton Theological Seminary, where he was awarded the First Maitland Prize in New Testament literature. He went on to minister Presbyterian churches in Washington State.

Most of the passengers who were injured in the crash of No. 106 from Cincinnati to Pittsburgh presumably recovered from their trauma, but Mrs. W.S. Greer was not so fortunate. The following item appeared, nearly two years after the wreck, in the August 8, 1890 edition of the *Dodge City Times*:

> *Mr. and Mrs. W.S. Greer desire to tender their sincere thanks to their many friends of Dodge City, for the many kindnesses shown during their recent misfortune; and also to the gentlemen employees of A.T. & S.F. R.R., for their donation of a beautiful pair of crutches, which will be used and appreciated during life.*

Train traffic in the city of Washington declined in the twenty-first century to not more than once a day. The diesel locomotives that haul freight cars back and forth to factories on the western side of town do not spew clouds of steam and coal smoke. They are not the breathing, chugging machines of old that announced their arrival and departure with the clanging of brass bells and the screams of steam whistles but instead clear the track with electric horns.

The modern, infrequent freight trains travel the same rails, however. They still pass the old station house built shortly after the famous train wreck and painstakingly restored a century later, still pass over West Maiden Street on the same trestle crossed by the Cannonball Express.

The glorious days of railroading are long gone. Yet we cannot escape these phantoms.

6
THE MURDER OF THELMA YOUNG

Most crimes, no matter how heinous and horrid, fade from the collective memory of a community after time. Names of killers and victims, gruesome details and emotional damage are seldom recalled a generation later by those not directly involved. But sometimes, and in some places, a brutal and ugly thing will not shake loose from the communal mind. It will not go away. Such is the murder of Thelma Young.

Few people living today can remember the events of late December 1927, but the teenager's slaying is still among the best-known crimes in Washington County history.

The Bellevue neighborhood in North Franklin Township is aptly named. Houses on Altamont Avenue, close to the city line, are perched like birds on wires overlooking Washington below, the factories and smokestacks to the west and the rolling waves of hills beyond them. Thelma Young, seventeen, wearing a tan checked coat, emerged at 7:00 p.m. on the night of Thursday, December 29, from the two-story frame house at 63 Altamont and headed into the cool, damp air, thick with mist.

Walking down Baltimore Avenue, she cut through the alley to Oregon Street. (Oregon is the street off West Maiden Street near All Ways Moving and Storage, and it turns into Mill Street after a short distance.) She continued left, passing under the Baltimore & Ohio Railroad bridge to West Wheeling Street and on into town. One of her older sisters, Mary Miller, was standing in front of the Washington Gardens dance hall on West Beau Street with her husband, Henry, and waved to her. Thelma stopped to talk.

Thelma Young's grave marker in Washington Cemetery. *Photo by Tim Warco.*

From inside the Gardens came strains of dance music from some of the most popular tunes of 1927: "Ain't She Sweet," "My Blue Heaven," "Blue Skies," "Me and My Shadow" and "Someone to Watch Over Me." Mary handed her little sister a copy of *True Romances* magazine and gave her some change to see a movie.

The posters at the Harris State Theatre on North Main Street advertised a holiday show featuring vaudeville acts, film shorts and a main feature, *The City Gone Wild*, starring Pittsburgh native Thomas Meighan. But Thelma walked by, turning left on Chestnut Street and into the Court for a screening of the silent film *Judgment of the Hills* with Frankie Darro, "the screen's greatest boy star," or so the marquee claimed.

An uncle, Wray Young, would testify years later that he saw Thelma on West Chestnut Street at 9:30 p.m., and they talked for a few minutes. A friend, Glen Stauffer, also stopped to talk with her a little farther down the street and last saw her at the corner of North Franklin and Chestnut.

Thelma walked south on Franklin and turned west on Wheeling. Jimmy Greco, watchman at the Pennsylvania Railroad crossing at West Wheeling Street, recognized her as she crossed the tracks at 10:10 p.m. He called out to her, and she replied cheerily, "Good evening!"

Greco watched as her figure disappeared into the fog. He was the last person to see Thelma Young alive.

At eight o'clock the next morning, a Baltimore Avenue resident called city police to report that a drunken woman was lying in the alley between

The Murder of Thelma Young

The alley from Oregon Street to Baltimore Avenue, as it appears today. *Photo by the author.*

Baltimore and Oregon Street. The alley, which is now paved, was more of a path at the time, used by residents of Bellevue as a shortcut. City police lieutenant Harvey Joliffe went to the alley and found the body of Thelma Young, nearly naked and covered in blood. He immediately called Washington County detective William Dinsmore.

A discarded copper washbasin was near the body, splattered with blood, and beside it was a brick, also bloodied. It was apparent that the girl's head had been struck a number of times, probably with the brick, and her throat was deeply bruised and gouged. Scattered in the wet, dead grass were a pair of shoes, a checked coat, underwear, a pin, a string of beads and an issue of *True Romances* magazine. They found footprints and the impression of a hand in the soft soil. About fifteen feet from where the corpse lay, Dinsmore picked up a large bone button, like those on a man's raincoat, and put it in his coat pocket.

Dinsmore's career had not been in police work. He had served in the Pennsylvania National Guard, Company H, 10th Infantry Regiment, which was sent in 1916 to the U.S.-Mexican border for the Pancho Villa campaign.

County detective William B. Dinsmore served as a lieutenant in Company H, 110th Infantry Regiment, in World War I. *Courtesy of Observer Publishing Co.*

Later, with Company H of the 110th Infantry, he fought in France during World War I. He nearly died after being gassed on the battlefield. When he finally recovered, he took a position as a detective in the Washington County District Attorney's Office.

Dinsmore photographed everything as it lay before collecting the items and arranging for removal of the body.

Pathologist George W. Ramsey performed an autopsy on Friday afternoon and determined the girl had been raped. She had been strangled, but he determined the cause of death was one of twelve blows to the head with a blunt instrument that had fractured her skull and created a three-inch gash above her eye. Even before he was finished with his examination, the public was already in a rage. The afternoon newspaper, the *Reporter*, had hit the streets with these banner headlines: "17-Year-Old Girl Brutally Murdered" and "Negro Youth Arrested as Suspect."

The newspaper described a desperate, futile fight the victim had waged to "save her honor" and the quick reaction by police:

> *Fred Drew, aged 17 years, arrested at his home at 162 Blaine Street, Kalorama, not far from the scene of the murder, is being held as a suspect. He was taken at his home by Chief of Police Joseph Verderber of the city force, and Private Arthur Flannigan, of the state police. It is understood that he was found there, hiding under the bed, and that when the officer dragged him out from that place, he said, "I did not do it, I did not do it, but I know who did do it."*

Drew was known as a neighborhood troublemaker with aspirations to become a burglar. When police grabbed him, he might have thought they were looking for him in regard to a recent break-in on East Wheeling Street, not for murder. At any rate, by the next day, police had discounted his role in the slaying and moved on to other suspects.

With glass and steel factories operating at full capacity, Washington had grown by 1927 to a city of twenty-five thousand. Along with the growth came crime, and police homicide investigations had become routine. During the early 1920s, the number of murders in the city was averaging twenty-five per year. "This has been due to the Black Hand, an organization which lives off tribute levied upon Italians, who are under the threat of death from the organization," wrote Earle Forrest in his *History of Washington County*, published in 1926. "Its members are expert gunmen, who seem to know no fear when they are ordered to kill some of their countrymen who have refused to pay tribute."

The murder of Thelma Young, however, was extraordinary, not just for its savagery but also for the innocence and circumstances of its victim. One of sixteen children of Sylvester and Iva Young, Thelma worked to help support her family, the previous summer as a maid at the Nease House hotel on South Main Street and through the autumn as a domestic in Washington & Jefferson College football team's training house near College Field, where she was well liked and considered a diligent worker.

The county commissioners immediately offered a $2,500 reward for information leading to the conviction of her killer. The outpouring of public sympathy, grief and anger might not have occurred if the victim had not been white or had been a foreigner. The local newspapers reported that Thelma, who wore her hair cut short and in permanent

Thelma Young, photographed in 1926 or 1927. *Courtesy of Thelma Jean Piatt.*

waves, as was the fashion, was friendly and outgoing and had a reputation as a good girl.

That she could die as she did took the town's breath away.

A Daunting Case

Police at the time of Thelma Young's murder relied on footwork, not science, in their investigations. Today, such a crime might have been quickly solved with DNA tests and laboratory analysis of blood, hair and other evidence. Chief Verderber's force, county detectives and the state police had no such resources and instead conducted countless hours of questioning. Dozens of witnesses were hauled in and grilled, then released. Among them were Ben Young and Thomas Garrett, who were having a conversation under a street lamp on Oregon Street at 10:00 p.m. the night of the murder. They parted just before Thelma came walking up the street. Garrett walked up the alley toward his home and might well have passed the murderer hiding in the darkness. Blood found on his cap and clothing was sent to Chicago for analysis and was determined to be from an animal.

Police had heard of a man running along the tracks from West Wheeling Street late on the night of the murder. The same man was reported to be hitching rides west on Route 40. They tracked him down in Wheeling but dismissed him as a suspect. Another lead that turned out to be false was the discovery of an abandoned, gore-spattered car in Maryland in which was found a bloody hammer.

After weeks of investigation turned into months, Ora Slater, a private detective from Cincinnati, was called in to assist. Slater had built a reputation as a brilliant crime solver. A year earlier, he had cracked the case of the murder of Canton newspaper editor Don Mellett, killed by order of a handful of mobsters and the Canton police chief for his campaign against corruption. Mellett received the Pulitzer Prize posthumously for his work. But Slater was unable to turn up anything new in Washington. He determined that the slaying was probably the work of a transient.

The anniversary of the murder passed, still without any new leads. Then, on April 26, 1928, Dinsmore, the county detective, received a call from the Allegheny County Workhouse. An inmate there, Clarence Klingingsmith, wanted to talk. Dinsmore had hoped to hear a confession, but the inmate instead implicated another man. The detective followed that trail, but it was a dead end.

The Murder of Thelma Young

A year later, in April 1929, a prisoner at the Ohio State Reformatory in Mansfield named Paul Girard, alias Hobbs, confessed to killing Thelma Young, but his story proved to be a fabrication.

Dinsmore brought a suspect back from North Carolina for questioning, and other investigators traveled to Washington, D.C., to interview a former W&J student, but both were cleared.

Years went by, and then, in December 1935, yet another Allegheny County Workhouse inmate claimed guilt. It was determined he was drunk when he confessed. His intention was to get back to the Washington County Jail in time for Christmas.

Clark Miller lived just a few houses away from Thelma Young's family on Altamont Avenue, and soon after he became a constable in January 1936, he began to receive complaints from women in the neighborhood who were being bothered on their way to and from town. As Ray Sprigle, a reporter for the *Pittsburgh Post-Gazette*, would recall in a 1949 feature article, "My Biggest Stories: The Beast Who Walked Like a Man":

> *Several women in his district complained to him that winter that big, truculent Bob Dreamer, a giant, 200-pound ape-like man, had accosted and in a couple of instances, mauled them. With little harm, except to their dignity. None of the women wanted to appear in court against him but they wanted Constable Miller to do something about it. He found that Dreamer had been following and annoying women for years.*

Dreamer lived at the top of steep Blaine Street in the neighborhood known as Kalorama. He was a railroad worker who was known to be odd or to have some kind of mental deficiency. Miller had known Dreamer, thirty-nine, for about twenty years. He knew that he had split from his wife, who was almost twenty years younger than her husband. And he remembered that Dreamer had befriended Thelma's brother Clyde.

Charles Tarr of Fulton Street told Miller he had seen Dreamer bothering women in the neighborhood, and he took this information to police. Dreamer's estranged wife, Mary, twenty-one years old, was brought to the state police barracks for questioning.

"Did he ever talk of having killed anyone?" she was asked.

DEATH CHAIR IS HIS FATE

This photograph of Robert Dreamer was first published by the *Reporter* on January 27, 1936, after his arrest. *Courtesy of Observer Publishing Co.*

"Only once," she replied. "We were out one night with another girl and he quarreled with her. He grabbed her by the throat half in fun. 'I'll fix you like I did Thelma,' he told her."

A warrant was issued for Dreamer's arrest. At 1:00 a.m. on January 21, Miller, chief county detective Mike Powell and Detective William McBride waited at the Pennsylvania Railroad freight station for Dreamer to arrive on the "bummer" train from Carnegie, where he had been working at the Scully railroad yards.

"Come with me," Powell said to Dreamer. "We'll take you home in a little while."

The trio took Dreamer to the state police barracks, where Sergeant William Hanna began to interrogate him. Four hours later, they knew they had their first solid suspect since the murder more than eight years earlier. Dreamer was packed into a patrol car and driven to the Canonsburg jail for further questioning.

Dreamer was confined for three and a half days to a seven- by ten-foot cell at the Canonsburg jail and given food—bologna and bread—once a day. He would testify at his trial later that year that he was deprived of sleep and water, beaten by a state trooper and questioned for long periods with his chair placed over a heating register. The only person in the jail he could talk to was a drunk who never uttered more than two words: "Sixty days."

Police insisted that Dreamer was not mistreated. Sergeant Hanna denied telling Dreamer, "You are not right up there [in the head]. It is going to be better for you to tell us everything." He also denied saying, "Bob, if you give us a statement, you will be away a couple of years and be back on the railroad. If you don't give us a statement, you'll be back in jail and rot there. If you don't give us a statement, we'll put the clampers on you."

Dreamer remained firm that he had nothing to do with the girl's death. Then, on January 24, a break came.

Ray Sprigle recalled the scene in his 1949 article:

> *He denied all until Hanna tossed a brown bone button on the desk in front of Dreamer.*
> *"Where did you get that?" Bob wanted to know.*
> *"Never mind where we got it. What about it?" Hanna demanded.*
> *"Why, I lost it. It's off my raincoat."*
> *"When did you lose it?"*
> *"Why, I guess the night Thelma was killed."*
> *That did it. That was the break.*
> *The button had been picked up at the scene of the murder of Thelma eight years before, plainly torn from her assailant's coat in her struggle to escape death.*

Dreamer was taken back to the state police barracks in Washington that morning. The next day, after a third consecutive night of record below-zero temperatures, a foot-thick blanket of snow lay on the ground. At 11:00 a.m., Dreamer was led into a room where a stenographer and nine officers and detectives awaited his statement.

In response to questions, mainly from Hanna and Dinsmore, called back from his recent retirement because of his familiarity with the case, Dreamer said that he had been working at the railroad roundhouse nearby. He left work and went to the alley leading from Oregon Street to Baltimore Avenue because he had seen a girl pass through there earlier. He said a girl came up the alley at 10:20 p.m.—he judged the time from a passing B&O freight train. He grabbed and tussled with her, hit her with a brick at least twice and then had sex with her twice. The first time, he said, she moaned a little; the second time she was silent and did not move.

Dreamer said that he had not intended to kill her. He returned to work, covering up scratches on his face and neck by tying a handkerchief around his neck. He left work at 2:30 a.m. and went directly to the Wayne Street home of his sister, with whom he was staying. He burned his clothing and his coat there. He went back to the scene of the killing at 4:30 a.m., saw the body and gathered up her dress, underwear and a shoe and burned them. He said that three days later, he noticed blood on his underwear, soaked them in lamp oil and burned them in the same place, on a hill behind the roundhouse where the Trinity High School track is now located.

The statement still exists in its original form. It is included in the case file of *Commonwealth v. Robert Dreamer*, kept in Washington County's storage building across Main Street from the courthouse. The transcript of his trial no longer exists. Oddly, parts of the statement of January 25 and another taken five days later in the office of District Attorney James C. Bane have been redacted; sections of questions and answers have been neatly clipped from it with scissors or a razor blade and removed.

A Swift Trial Expected

The arrest of Big Bob Dreamer came as a shock, not just to neighbors who knew him as a friendly, hard worker who would do odd jobs and haul coal when not employed by the railroad, but also to the Young family.

"It most certainly was a surprise to the entire family," said Iva Young, Thelma's mother, in an interview with the *Observer* shortly after Dreamer's arrest. "Why, I can recall now that one of my sons said Robert Dreamer bought a newspaper from him the morning the story came out about Thelma's death and stood on the corner near where she was killed and read about it."

Thelma's father, Sylvester, a glassworker, said, "He always appeared to me to be a nice sort of fellow. I do recall he acted perhaps queer at times but never thought anything about it."

The local newspapers predicted a speedy trial, and District Attorney Bane, detectives and police were confident of a conviction. The voluntary, signed confession of the defendant was a damning piece of evidence, even if it was the only solid evidence they possessed.

Others were more cautious. Some Bellevue residents wondered if the Bob Dreamer they knew was either smart enough or evil enough for murder.

Some wondered if a confession was enough proof of the man's guilt in that many such statements were later repudiated or shown to be forced on the accused by police. Furthermore, the court had appointed Thomas Christman, an experienced criminal attorney, to be Dreamer's lawyer. Christman had defended Ray Kunselman in another high-profile murder trial just six months earlier. That jury found Kunselman guilty in the death of Dorothy Horne but had declined to impose the death penalty. That jury's determination of murder in the first degree was somewhat surprising in light of Christman's spirited defense. The Young family was also not so confident in the commonwealth's case, so they hired local attorney Wray Zelt to serve as special prosecutor.

Shortly after 3:00 p.m. on Tuesday, May 12, 1936, Judge Howard Hughes concluded another homicide trial and called for a twenty-minute recess, after which the trial of Robert Dreamer would begin. Jury selection went slowly. Of the first seventy-one prospective jurors interviewed, thirty-seven were dismissed because they opposed the death penalty. Finally, late on Thursday morning, the panel was completed with eight men of various occupations and four women, all described as housekeepers.

The formal arraignment took place after jury selection. "Wearing a new blue suit, blue shirt and tie, Dreamer presented a neat appearance," the *Observer* reported. "He has grown a mustache during his stay in jail. Except for the usual prison pallor, the burly defendant does not show any effects of more than two months of confinement. Seemingly he was in good spirits."

When asked for his plea, Dreamer faced the jury and, in a clear, loud voice, said, "Not guilty." Special Prosecutor Zelt then made his opening remarks, briefly detailing the actions of the defendant on the night more than eight years earlier and asking jurors to do their duty and send Dreamer to the electric chair.

Seated beside him at the defense table was one of Dreamer's seven sisters: Gladys Chase, who intended to be with him throughout the trial. Three other sisters were also in the courtroom. On the opposite side of the gallery sat the mother of the victim, Iva Young, and one of the girl's sisters, Mary Miller. Also in the courtroom was Dreamer's estranged wife, Mary. She had filed charges against her husband in February 1935 for desertion and nonsupport.

One of the spectators in Courtroom No. 1 had a special and professional interest in the testimony that was to follow. Frank Ritz, chief detective for Allegheny County, was anxious for the proceedings to conclude because, regardless of the outcome, he intended to charge Dreamer with the murder of another girl.

More Than One Victim?

On the night of January 18, 1936, just two days before Robert Dreamer was picked up for questioning about the death of Thelma Young, fifteen-year-old Elizabeth Louden did not return as expected to her home in Walker's Mill, about two miles west of Heidelberg in Allegheny County.

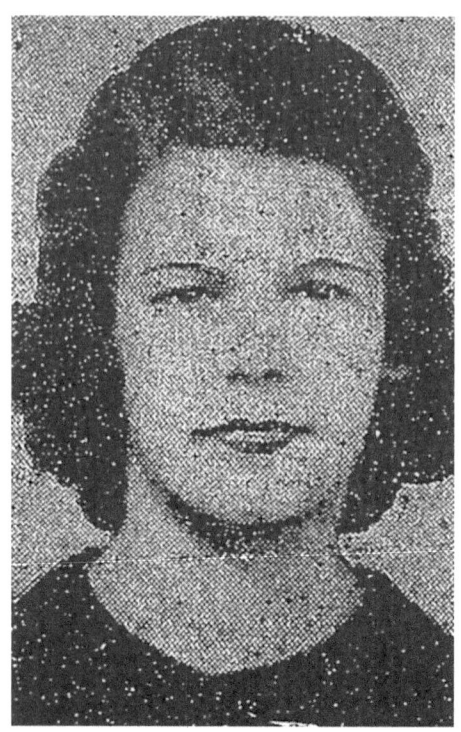

Elizabeth Louden.

A search turned up nothing, and police were inclined to believe she had run away. A few days later, a blizzard hit the area and covered the ground with more than a foot of snow, followed by a severe cold snap. Six weeks later, when the snow melted, an umbrella, purse and coat belonging to the girl were found on the lawn of a house on Noblestown Road in nearby Rennersdale. The next day, her naked body, still locked in ice, was discovered in Walker's Run. She had been raped and strangled. There were five holes from an instrument like a miner's pick in her skull. Teeth marks were clearly visible on her lip and cheek.

John Herleman, a twenty-six-year-old parolee who had been seeing the girl, was immediately suspected, but his alibi was solid. Scores of other suspects were questioned and ruled out.

At the time Elizabeth Louden's body was found, Thelma Young had been dead for more than eight years, and her suspected killer was in jail and awaiting trial. The details of her murder had long been forgotten; no one recognized the similarities between the two slayings. No one in Allegheny law enforcement made the connection, but *Post-Gazette* reporter Ray Sprigle did. He recalled that Robert Dreamer was a railroad worker, and a large railway switching facility was near where the Louden girl was killed:

> *The Scully Yards are within easy reach of Carnegie and Walker's Mill on its outskirts. Dreamer worked there January 16 and 17. He failed to show for work on the 18th and 19th. He was back at work January 20. I checked with bartenders and found that Dreamer was a well known figure in Carnegie saloons and had a record of having mauled several women in tavern backrooms.*

The Murder of Thelma Young

> *Girlfriends and family of Elizabeth Louden told me that Elizabeth had told them several times she had been followed by a "tall, dark man, always with his coat collar turned up and his hat brim pulled down." That was Dreamer in life.*

Sprigle wrote a story pinning the murder on Dreamer. He was afraid to get himself too far out on a limb. "I attributed my Sherlocking to 'law officers in two counties.'" The story appeared in the March 13 *Post-Gazette* and irritated Ritz. But the detective knew that the reporter was on to something.

Over the next two months, Ritz found eight witnesses who saw Dreamer in Carnegie on the day Elizabeth was killed. Two of them were drinking at a bar with him in Walker's Mill that night and said he left for two hours and returned disheveled and excited. He found a Carnegie waitress who claimed Dreamer beat and choked her when she refused to go to Washington with him. He found inmates at the Washington jail who said Dreamer bragged about killing the girl, and he took impressions of Dreamer's teeth to compare to the marks left on the victim's cheek.

Ritz figured that the icing on the cake would be a murder conviction of Dreamer by a Washington County jury. And as he listened to the long list of prosecution witnesses testify, the chances of that looked pretty good.

Whom to Believe?

On Thursday, May 14, District Attorney Bane took the witness stand and was asked to read Dreamer's statement of January 25. Before he could do so, Judge Hughes ordered all those under sixteen years old to be taken out of the courtroom so that they might be spared hearing the shocking details of the crime. Bane read the confession to a hushed courtroom, which, when Bane had finished, froze in awkward silence for several seconds. Few present then could imagine the jury reaching any other verdict than guilty.

If that weren't enough, there was the business of the button. Dreamer claimed to have burned his coat the morning after the murder, so it could not be proven to be his, except that he acknowledged that it was.

The defense opened its case on Friday. Dreamer repudiated his confession and said investigators had cajoled and tricked him into making it. The writer for the *Reporter* took note of the defendant's demeanor on the stand: "That Dreamer does not realize the seriousness of his crime is very apparent. He smiled and laughed, just as he might in having a conversation with a friend."

Attorney Christman attacked the supposed confession and all of the evidence. As he would tell the jury in his closing arguments on Tuesday, the plaster casts of the handprint found beside the body and that of Dreamer's right hand did not match. Sergeant Hanna admitted that he had not taken measurements of the hand and print and that he had never made such a cast before. Christman pointed out that the clothing put before the bar was never entered as evidence and that it contained a coat, dress, shoes and underwear. He reminded jurors that Dreamer claimed in his statement to have burned her dress, a shoe and underwear.

Christman further picked apart the confession with witnesses. L.W. Mumbower, who worked with Dreamer at the roundhouse, said Dreamer was not wearing a handkerchief and did not have scratches on his face and neck at the end of his shift, and Ollie Knestrick, Dreamer's supervisor, said Dreamer could not have been gone from work that night more than fifteen minutes without him knowing about it.

When Dreamer was on the witness stand, Christman asked him, "Bob, did you kill Thelma Young?"

"I did not," Dreamer replied.

"Did you ever attack Thelma Young?"

"I did not," Dreamer answered. "I can say that with a clear conscience. I never saw Thelma Young that I know of."

The jurors adjourned to the George Washington Hotel to deliberate at 2:20 p.m. on Tuesday, May 19. They returned two hours and forty minutes later to a nearly empty courtroom with their verdict. Samuel Yohe, the foreman, stated they found Robert Dreamer guilty as charged and recommended the penalty of death.

Dreamer stood motionless, his mouth half open, gazing intently at the jury. His sister, Gladys Chase, who had sat beside him for every moment of the weeklong trial, was stunned. "She gazed at the floor, striving hard to restrain herself," the *Observer* reported, "but in spite of this tears coursed down her cheeks."

Later, after Dreamer was returned to the jail, the newspaper stated, "he seemed little concerned over the death sentence and…he ate heartily when given his evening meal."

The following day, Dreamer's lawyer filed a petition for a new trial. Meanwhile, a coroner's jury met in Allegheny County for an inquest in the murder of Elizabeth Louden. Much to Detective Ritz's chagrin, the jury found only that the girl had met her death at the hands of a person or persons unknown. That jury apparently did not believe Dreamer's fellow prisoners and other characters who testified that they heard him brag about killing her. Without a confession, Dreamer would not be charged.

THE LONG WALK

The petition for a new trial was denied. Christman appealed to the Pennsylvania Supreme Court in November 1936, arguing that photographs of the body of Thelma Young introduced as evidence had prejudiced the jury. On December 3, the high court affirmed the verdict of the lower court, with Justice George W. Maxey writing, "The photographs did not convict the defendant."

This photograph published in the *Reporter* on the day of his execution shows Robert Dreamer shortly after his arrest on January 21, 1936. *Courtesy of Observer Publishing Co.*

On December 21, a warrant was issued for Dreamer's execution. On January 27, 1937, the Pennsylvania Pardons Board—Dreamer's last hope—denied his application, and two days later, Sheriff Fred Brady told Dreamer they would leave Washington County Jail for Rockview State Penitentiary in Bellefonte the following morning. Brady advised him, "You know, you always wanted to look good, Bob."

"Yes, I know I did," he replied, his eyes watering and his voice beginning to shake.

As they left the following morning, Dreamer shook hands with prisoners and guards, and it was apparent he had followed the sheriff's advice. He was wearing a neat dark blue suit, tan shirt, brown tie and gray felt hat. He was smoking a cigar, one from a box given to him by a friend the previous day.

The prisoner still held some hope that Governor George H. Earle would intervene and stop the execution, and his lawyer, citing that

Dreamer had the mind of an eight-year-old, appealed for him to do so. But Earle had never overruled his pardons board, and he wasn't about to start with this case.

Arriving at Rockview, Dreamer was questioned for the last time about the murders of both Thelma Young and Elizabeth Louden. His final statement was, "I had nothing to do with either one of the cases and if you execute me you will execute an innocent man."

"Big Bob Dreamer was one man I wanted to watch die," wrote Ray Sprigle in his 1949 remembrance. "All my life I've hated sex murderers and the maudlin fools who weep for them. I had to hurry to keep the date with Bob, though. Two days before he was to die I was in Louisville covering the big 1937 flood. I had to fly back to Pittsburgh by way of Chicago."

Sprigle watched Dreamer go to his death a half hour after midnight on February 1, 1937. Following is his account:

> *While we waited to see a man die, old Bob Elliott, the executioner who had killed more than a thousand men and women in his time and had never served a day for it, fiddled with the deadly tools of his trade. There, as always, was his old galvanized wash tub where he soaked the sponges of the deadly electrodes that had burned the life out of more than 200 men and one woman...*
>
> *At his switchboard he threw his lever and the row of lights leaped into brilliance that cut through the glare of the ceiling flood lamps. The prison doctor stepped up beside the chair to direct a little speech to the group of us seated on the massive concrete pews facing the chair. The lights, he told us, indicated that the mechanism of the chair was in working order...*
>
> *The door from the death cells—the "dancing floor," they call it at Sing Sing—opened with scarcely a sound. Now Bob Dreamer was on his way to die, life measured in steps now.*
>
> *He shuffled into the execution room, his giant stature dwarfing the burley guards, one on either side, gripping his arms. We could hear the scrape of his feet on the concrete above the sound of the labored breathing of those who were to kill him and those who were to watch him die...*
>
> *The giant killer blinked dazedly as he came through the last door but one. He was like a giant stuffed doll as the guards backed him into the chair and his knees let him down. Swiftly the guards shackled him fast, legs and arms. And the great wide strap across his chest. Now, the greasy looking leathern black cap that so many have worn so briefly before him, its wet electrode in its crown tight against the close-clipped skull.*

> At his switchboard Old Bob moves swiftly and surely and nimbly for one so old. One last quick glance at the man he is about to kill and the veined, gnarled old hand throws the switch. The giant figure surges against its bonds with a crash and the great chair creaks. With his other hand old Bob fiddles with the rheostat. "Heatin' 'im and coolin' 'im," the guard puts it.
>
> Bob pulls the switch and the giant hulk slumps in a heap. But the Commonwealth isn't finished with this killer yet. Twice more Old Bob throws his switch and plays delicately with his rheostat. Each time the 200 pounds of dead meat on the broad seat seems to come to life again. The last time Old Bob waits until a curl of smoke corkscrews upward from under the black cap. He pulls the switch for the last time. With fingers that never tremble or make a false move, he unfastens the two top buttons of Dreamer's shirt, bares the wide chest, flaming red now, and visibly radiating heat—or at least it seems that way. The prison physician steps forward and plants his stethoscope on that vast expanse of hot skin. He listens, moves his stethoscope about, pulls the shirt together again, announces that this man is dead.
>
> The guards unshackle the body, grunt as they heave it onto the wheeled table and shove it swiftly into the little autopsy room—where in brief seconds the autopsy is under way.
>
> Well, Big Bob Dreamer had paid for his first murder. And had gotten the second one for free. There was nothing more that anyone could do for him.

During the autopsy, Dr. John Weixel noted the severe damage to internal organs caused by the two thousand volts of electricity. He also discovered an old injury: a fractured skull.

Unforgiven, Unforgotten

None of Thelma Young's brothers or sisters is still living or able to tell about it, but the children of those siblings recall the stories.

Thelma Jean Piatt was born four years after the killing, a daughter of the victim's sister Beaulah. "My aunt, Romaine, slept with Thelmie, that's what they called her. On that night she didn't come home, well, they didn't have a telephone, they just thought she had stayed over at a girlfriend's.

"My mother never talked much about it. I think she didn't want to frighten us. But she never let us go more than a block away from our house," Mrs. Piatt said.

"I remember Bob Dreamer," said Clyde "Chig" Young, the son of Thelma's brother Clyde.

"Dreamer was my father's best friend. I was seven years old when he was executed. He was over at the house all the time. He was a big man, must have been over six feet tall and had fourteen-inch shoes. I remember—I must have been five or six—my brother and I would sit on his feet and ride them around the house," Young said.

"I remember they were selling extra papers on the street the day he was killed," he added.

Young's father was eighteen at the time Thelma was killed. After that, the family would dress him in girl's clothing and have him walk at night along the alley to try to lure the killer.

"My uncle Howard walked through that alley where she was killed at about 4:00 a.m. that night, but he was so drunk he didn't notice anything. He said he could remember seeing a red coat on the ground, and he felt so bad that he didn't do anything but go home. But he couldn't have done anything. She was gone by then."

Young's uncles Howard and Herb were the oldest and used to go to brothels in Wheeling with Dreamer. He was known to be rough with the girls, but it never occurred to them that he could have been Thelma's killer. "All that time they spent together, my dad never suspected him," Young said.

The story of Thelma Young's murder did not end with the execution of Robert Dreamer.

About four weeks after his brother's trial for murder, William Dreamer, a twenty-nine-year-old divorced farmer, went missing from his father's West Finley Township home. Friends, neighbors and county and township officers conducted an extensive search but could not find him. Later, officers presumed he had gone west to live with relatives.

Five weeks later, on July 29, 1936, John Dreamer, father of Robert and William, was mowing in the orchard behind his house and had stopped to cut off the branch of a low-hanging tree that was in his way when, in tall grass beside the tree, he discovered his son's skeletal remains. A single-barreled shotgun lay across what had been his chest. The top of the head had been blown off. The coroner ruled the fatal blast was self-inflicted.

Big Bob Dreamer. *Illustration by the author.*

Almost a year later, on June 2, 1937, tragedy would call again. At 2:00 a.m., John William Dreamer, age sixty-seven, father of the executed man, died of a shotgun blast to the heart. Deputy Coroner R.A. Brownlee was told that the man had not been well and had become despondent. He ruled the death a suicide.

John, William and Robert are all buried in the family plot in Salem Methodist Cemetery, West Finley Township.

Although the coroner's reports concerning the two deaths were never officially questioned, some Young family members have another explanation. They think that Thelma's two oldest brothers, Herbert and Howard, were responsible.

"I don't believe they did it, though," Clyde Young said of his uncles. "This was during the Depression, and these guys were lucky to work one or two days a week in the glass factory. They didn't have any money. Where would they get a car to go out there and do a thing like that?"

Tim Warco, the current Washington County coroner and a grandson of Beaulah Young, disagrees, however. His says his uncle Donald Young gave him a single-barreled shotgun and told him it was the same gun that killed both men.

Six months after the trial, Clark Miller, the constable who gathered the information that led to Dreamer's arrest, sued the county for the reward that had been offered by the commissioners the day after Thelma Young's murder. On September 3, 1938, Miller was granted the $2,500 reward.

The law enforcement community was never in doubt that it had secured the conviction of the right man. No one was ever charged with Elizabeth Louden's murder, and nothing ever occurred in the Washington area to suggest that Thelma Young's killer was still alive. The button, they believed, was the proof of Dreamer's guilt. He knew that he had lost it; he had searched for it many times, and when he was shown it so many years later, he recognized it as his. That's when he—not bright enough to realize that his coat no longer existed and that the button could not be tied to him—began to spill the truth.

Doubt, however, is an awfully hard thing to eradicate. And for most women, walking alone at night would never be without fear and worry.

And for good reason. Other women would be raped and others would be murdered, though their cases might never become as sensational as this one. Fifty years after Thelma's murder, Washington County would be gripped by fear, grief and anger again with the rape and murder of four young women within six months of one another in various parts of the county. Susan Rush, twenty-one, was killed on November 26, 1977, and Brenda Lee Ritter, eighteen, died on February 14, 1978. Both had been raped and strangled with parts of their clothing, and both murders remain unsolved.

Other sensational cases since that time have resulted in first-degree murder convictions and sentences of death. But Robert Dreamer has a particular distinction. He was the last person from Washington County to be executed.

BIBLIOGRAPHY

Batchelor, Captain Charles W. *Incidents in the Life of Chas. W. Batchelor.* Pittsburgh, PA: Joseph Eichbaum & Co., 1887.

Branton, Harriet. *Focus on Washington County.* Vols. 1–4. Washington, PA: Observer Publishing Co., 1979, 1980, 1982, 1984.

Caldwell's Illustrated Historical Centennial Atlas of Washington County, PA. Pittsburgh, PA: Otto Krebs, 1876.

Canonsburg Daily Notes, March 13, 25, 1936; May 21, 1936.

Commemorative and Biographical Record of Washington County, PA. Chicago: J.H. Beers and Co., 1893.

Connellsville (PA) Daily Courier, October 26, 1888; May 8, 1896.

Connors, Patrick. *Historic Towns of Washington County*. Monongahela, PA: Historic Towns Publishing, n.d.

Creigh, Alfred. *History of Washington County from Its First Settlement to the Present Time.* Harrisburg, PA: B. Singerly, Printer, 1905.

Bibliography

Crumrine, Boyd. *History of Washington County.* Philadelphia: L.H. Everts, 1882.

Daily Republican [Monongahela, PA], June 30, 1896.

Dodge City (KS) Times, August 8, 1890; November 28, 1890.

Forrest, Earle R. *History of Washington County*. Chicago: S.J. Clarke Publishing Co., 1926.

History of Washington County. Vols. 2 and 3. Chicago: S.J. Clarke Publishing Co., 1926.

McFarland, J.F. *Twentieth Century History of Washington County*. Chicago: Richmond-Arnold Publishing Co., 1910

Observer, October 25, 1888; July 18, 20, 21, 1891; October 10, 16, 18–21, 1891; February 16–24, 1892; May 19–21, 1892; August 8, 1892; February 4–7, 19, 20, 1907; December 30, 31, 1927; May 29, 1928; June 14–17, 1935; November 19–25, 1935; January 27, 1936; May 13–21, 1936; July 30, November 24, 1936; June 3, 1937; December 28, 1937; March 1, 1938; July 18, 21, 1941.

Pittsburgh Dispatch, August 7, 1892.

Pittsburgh Post-Gazette, March 27, 1936; April 10, 1949.

Pittsburgh Press, October 27, 1926; November 19, 24, 1935; April 28, 1936; May 22, 1936; December 22, 1936.

Polk's Washington City Directory. Pittsburg, PA: R.L. Polk & Co., 1896, 1902, 1903, 1906, 1911, 1915, 1929, 1935, 1939, 2013.

Reporter, October 19–25, 1888; July 17–21, 1891; October 10, 1891; February 15–24, 1892; May 19–21, 1892; August 8, 1892; February 2–9, 18–20, 26, 1907; March 9, 1907; April 15, 1907; March 13, 1926; December 29–31, 1927; June 20, 22, 1928; June 13–17, 1935; November 18–25, 1935; December 7, 1935; May 12–20, 1936; January 29–31, 1937; February 1, 1937; September 3, 8, 1937; October 4, 1941.

BIBLIOGRAPHY

Tibbetts, John C. *The American Theatrical Film: Stages in Development.* N.p.: Popular Press, 1985.

White, Alvin Dinsmore. *Historic Sketches of Northern Washington County.* Washington County, PA, 1979.

ABOUT THE AUTHOR

A Parker Burroughs has been a newspaper writer and editor for more than four decades and is the retired executive editor of the *Observer-Reporter* in Washington, Pennsylvania. He has worked as a consultant to newspapers in Russia and Ukraine and has taught writing at Bethany College. He is the editor of *200 Years: Our History Through the Pages of the* Observer-Reporter and author of *Enter, With Torches: Recollections of a Grumpy Old Editor*. He and his wife, artist Alice McClenathan Burroughs, live in Washington.

Visit us at
www.historypress.net
....
This title is also available as an e-book

www.ingramcontent.com/pod-product-compliance
Lightning Source LLC
Chambersburg PA
CBHW042143160426
43201CB00022B/2392